To Look Upward: One Flight Instructor's Journey

Rob Mixon

ISBN-10: **1545052301**
ISBN-13: **978-1545052303**

DEDICATION

This book is dedicated to all my students, as well as all of those having gone through or are experiencing, their own surreal world of abuse.

CONTENTS

ACKNOWLEDGMENTS

A special thanks to my wife Linda for her patience in the writing of this book and my uncle Charles Wesley Price, Jr., Family Historian, and Rick Mixon, Airframe and Power Plant Mechanic who is excellent in aerobatic flying and airshow announcing.

INTRODUCTION

My career as a Flight Instructor began early when, as a boy growing up in Florida, I and my mother would welcome home my father, a Pan American Airways pilot returning from far away exotic places. I was always eager to hear about these places, and my father didn't disappoint. These stories were to shape my early life until I became a Certified Flight Instructor. Slowly turning the pages of my pilot log books, I see the names of students spanning over fifty-four years and 20,000 hours of flight time. In the remarks, procedures, maneuvers, and endorsements section of the books belonging to my students, the endorsements were signed by me, Robert G. Mixon 1585409 CFI, ATP, as well Multiengine Sea, Multiengine Land, Single-engine Land, and Glider Ratings, but the certifications don't tell the whole story. Perhaps even more important is how a Certified Flight Instructor can change the lives of others using the airplane to build confidence and humility. The realization that perhaps it is not the Certified Flight Instructor or the airplane who makes this change but a Higher Power is ridiculous to many, strange to some, but, in the truth that follows, you may find it appropriate. "Those who wait for the Lord shall renew their strength; they shall mount up with wings like eagles; they shall run and not be weary; they shall walk and not faint" (Isaiah 40:31).

This is a true story of survival of the body as well the heart and soul.

CHAPTER ONE

My father's plane would come plowing through the water with the deep throated roar of the huge four engines echoing off the walls of the terminal building. Pan American World Airways "Clipper Ships" in 1934. Capacity included 37 day passengers or 14 sleeper berths. Celebrities like Winston Churchill and famous Hollywood movie stars flew to exotic places in the S-42 seaplane even before land bases were constructed throughout South and Central America as well as Hawaii and Europe.

The date was April 11, 1936. Pan American Airways Puerto Rican Clipper, a four engine S-42 flying boat, was taking off from the harbor in Port of Spain, Trinidad. The flight engineer and captain had applied take off power. The four 660-horsepower supercharged engines roared as they came to life pushing the flight crew back into their seats.

The Puerto Rican Clipper raced across the surface of the harbor as it began to feel light in the water riding on the step on the bottom of the hull. A spray of salt water splashed over the cockpit windshield for a short time. Captain Henderson felt the control yoke and rudder pedals become lighter as the seaplane slowly lifted off the surface of the harbor.

Suddenly, directly in front of the plane, a small commercial fishing boat appeared. Immediately, Captain Henderson applied full left rudder. He turned the control yoke completely to the left to maneuver the S-42 around the fishing boat. The right pontoon on the wing tip struck the boat causing the boat and plane to overturn. Both plane and boat mingled into a sinking pile of rubble. Three of the twenty-five on board the aircraft, including Captain Henderson, were killed.

On October 3, 1941, a Pan American Flight 203 Dominican Clipper, a flying boat, was flying a final approach to a water landing in San Juan Harbor, Puerto Rico. The surface of the water was crystal clear making for a perfect smooth-as-glass landing. Those conditions made the surface of the water invisible. The flight engineer and captain established a slow, power on, controlled descent. Just enough power was applied to allow the S-42 to slowly descend toward the surface of the harbor. The plane continued its slow descent in what seemed to be only inches above the transparent surface. The plane seemed to hang in the air as the captain became impatient lowering the nose of the Dominican Clipper toward the surface of the water. The plane plowed into the surface moving sideways in a nose low attitude.

The captain pulled back on the control yoke and added full power. But there was not enough flying speed, and the plane swerved violently to the right. The right wing plowed under the surface of the water. The Dominican Clipper immediately broke apart.

Of the twenty-seven people on board, the only two fatalities were the captain and co-pilot. The captain was John Henderson's younger brother Captain Donald Henderson. The co-pilot was a new hire whom my father had never met. The loss of his close friends, John and Don Henderson, weighed heavily on his mind and heart. He became overly conscientious about his mechanical responsibilities for keeping the flight crews and his passengers safe.

My father had never known his father. Furthermore, he lost his mother at an early age during the birth of his youngest sister. My father and his four sisters were suddenly homeless, so he moved in with a family who had a milk route, the Fassell family. Their son was Dante Fassel who later became a United States Congressman from Florida's 19th District.

When he was old enough to drive, he was assigned his own milk truck route. The old truck he drove was missing a fender, had rust on the hood, faded paint, and an engine that at times refused to run. He saw that truck as a great opportunity to sharpen his mechanical ability. Every time he rescued it, he felt as if he, too, had been rescued and became part of his new family.

1932

"Grady! When you wake up, get up! And when you get up, wake up!" were the first words he heard each morning for his 4:30 morning milk run. What started as a natural ability to keep a dilapidated milk truck running turned into the opportunity to use his mechanical abilities to be employed by Pan American World Airways in their seaplane base at Dinner Key in Coconut Grove, Florida.

My father used to poke around the bottom of the hull of those huge seaplanes as an apprentice aircraft cleaner. From the dirty, damp, bilges of the seaplanes, he moved up into the fabric shop learning how to cover aircraft control surfaces. The sheet metal shop came next where he learned how to form a flat piece of aluminum around the engine cowl using only hand tools. He turned flat pieces of aluminum into an engine cowl, banging and shaping them, amid the strong smell of burnt engine oil, aviation fuel, and aircraft dope. He finally worked his way through each of the shops in the large, silver metal hangars of Pan American World Airways. The salty sea breeze blowing up from the nearby water of Biscayne Bay was always welcome as it blew into the large open hangar doors.

This was long before the creation of the Occupational Safety and Health Administration (OSHA), so spraying things like spraying aircraft fabric with aircraft dope before a certified spray booth requiring fans and ventilation were not even thought of. It was not uncommon to see the airline mechanics leaving the hangars to breathe some fresh air, catching their breath as they lay outside on the top of the seawall.

When the huge four-engine S-42 seaplanes arrived, after the passengers deplaned, if the plane was scheduled for maintenance, it would be met by the "beaching crew." They would wade out into the water with a huge wheeled dolly, placing it under the floating hull because the seaplane had no landing gear or wheels. A strong cable was attached to a hook on the bottom and aft section of the hull called a "pelican hook." The plane would be made ready to be pulled backwards up the seaplane ramp out of the water and into the maintenance hangars. The hull design allowed for a seaplane to "get up on the step" during the takeoff. The "step" extended slightly lower than the last part of the hull, causing the hull to rest out of the water and allowing the plane to pick up speed for flight.

After completing his internship in each of Pan Am's maintenance shops, he was in the engine overhaul shop when he heard that they were hiring Flight Engineers. With his Airframe and Power Plant Mechanic license, he was qualified for the position and was accepted as a Flight Engineer on the S-42 seaplane. One important part of his job was to make repairs in remote locations. He used some pretty clever ways to make sure those old seaplanes could fly back home to Dinner Key, Florida.

On one trip to the remote Amazon jungle town of Belem, he had to use his ingenuity to repair a hole punched through the fuselage by a log during a water landing. Since there was no suitable material available, he solved the problem by riveting a Coca Cola sign to the outside of the hull showing the red logo just at the water line of the S-42 as it water taxied back into the harbor and terminal at Coconut Grove. I remember my mother laughing and pointing to my father's plane as it drifted up to the terminal dock. Seeing the bright Coca Cola letters, my mother named that flight "The Coca Cola Rescue Flight."

My mother came from a very colorful, complicated family. Her grandfather taught school in Mobile, Alabama where he became infatuated with a woman who worked in a bar with a complimentary job working upstairs, sleeping with men, to supplement her income. He fell more deeply in love with her, and wanted to marry her to get her out of that lifestyle. He apparently had a rival. A fight ensued and the rival was killed. The rival's uncle was the law in Mobile, and he set out to catch my mother's grandfather. All things considered, moving quickly to Florida would be a good move.

Without giving notice to the school where he taught, he packed up and moved all the way to Tampa, Florida, without the girl in Mobile. He did not want to be recognized as a teacher in case he had been followed. He worked odd jobs and stayed away from teaching jobs until things calmed down. After some time, he applied and got his Florida Teacher's Certificate.

He looked around Tampa for employment as a teacher, but there were no openings available. In his search of private schools, he came across a church that employed a young lady who taught Sunday School and taught children with special needs. The church did not have the money to hire him. He took a liking to this young lady whose name was Henrietta Boyett. She was beautiful, well educated, and from a prominent Tampa family.

After a serious courtship, he won the young lady's heart and was well received by her family. They married in 1884 and a son, Charles Wesley, was born on September 8, 1885. Henrietta was quite religious and named their son after the British evangelist John Wesley who had established the Methodist church.

Charles Henry Price started teaching in small Florida towns like Turkey Creek. It seemed he was paid one dollar per student per semester. Since the students had to help their parents on the farms, a semester lasted only four months.

In 1875, when not teaching, he ran excursions through the Okefenokee swamp along the Florida-Georgia border. At times, his customers included Teddy Roosevelt and U.S. House of Representatives William Bryant Jennings.

Moving to Coconut Grove, Florida, his son, Charles Wesley Price, had three sons and one daughter: Charles Wesley Price, Jr.; William T. Price; George Price, and Ida May Price, whose last name was changed to Mixon when she married my father.

Ida May was more of a tomboy than most girls, always playing rough with the boys by climbing trees and just getting into the usual childhood trouble.

One Sunday morning, she attended services at the Plymouth Congregational Church in Coconut Grove, Florida. She was up to her usual pranks. The church's architecture was designed like the Spanish missions of Mexico. It has been said that many of the huge beams on the ceiling in the church were savaged from old sailing ships that had run aground in Biscayne Bay's shallow waters. The who's who of Coconut Grove attended Plymouth Congregational Church.

Ida May was sitting in the back of the huge church with her brothers and parents on the front row. She reached into the pocket of her dress and pulled out a handful of marbles. The church went quiet in prayer. She put the marbles on the slanted wooden planked floor. The marbles began rolling over the uneven planks of wood toward her brothers and the front of the church. Click. Click. Click. Click. The sounds of the marbles kept going until they ended up at the feet of the preacher. Since there was no way to identify the culprit, my mother remained anonymous.

Charles Wesley Price, Jr. was always with his father, even at work. Once his father took him to work when the boy was five years old and they were working on a roofing job together. The owner of the building told the senior Price, "That boy is your responsibility." "He always is" came the reply. Charles Wesley Price, Sr. built apartments on 2756 Day Avenue in Coconut Grove. He also built the first water tower for Coconut Grove. He was also a blacksmith at Ann Hardee's Blacksmith Shop where he shod mules, making ten cents an hour or one dollar a day. He would rest the mule's leg on his as he sat on a stool to work. The mule would relax its leg, pushing its full weight against Price. When it became too heavy, Price, Sr. would pick up a stick he kept nearby and hit the mule just hard enough to make it tense. The mule would move its weight off his leg.

When Price, Sr. was building apartments and the water tower, his brother, William T. Price, established the first cement plant in Miami as well as the W.T. Price Dredging Company.

In 1921 W.T. Price Dredging Company dug a four-acre coral rock quarry. That same quarry became Venetian Pool, the public swimming pool of Coral Gables. It was developed with a Mediterranean Revival style with coral rock ornamental features including a Venetian-style bridge. At times, the pool was drained so the quarry's natural acoustical qualities were utilized for the Miami Symphony to perform.

My earliest memory of my mother was her standing in front of my high chair. The breeze from Biscayne Bay inflated the sheer white curtains by the open window where she was standing. The curtains puffed out looking like huge billowing white sails to a small child sitting in his high chair. The gentle breeze brushed back Mother's shoulder length brown hair exposing and framing her loving dark brown eyes. Her eyes sparkled as she picked up a baby spoon from the small tray in front of me. The baby spoon, filled with food, would "fly" out of the small jar as mother made an airplane noise circling over my head! "Open the hangar door!" she would say, momentarily stopping the airplane sound, as the "airplane" with its cargo of baby food would fly into my mouth.

Each time the spoon was empty I would prepare for the next "flight" as Mother would sing her happy, special song, "Praise God from whom all blessings flow; praise God all creatures here below." Her song would end just in time for another spoon of baby food to fly into the hangar.

Sometimes, we were filled with excitement when my father was coming home from a flight. At the Pan Am's seaplane terminal, there was an observation deck on the top where we would watch and wait. My father's plane would come plowing through the water with the deep-throated roar of the huge four engines echoing off the walls of the terminal building.

It was so exciting even to a young child. The sound of those strong radial engines filled my world with the anticipation of seeing my father.

"There he is! There he is!" Mother would shout holding me up over the wall surrounding the observation deck so that my father could see me. We would wave to each other. Then with my mother holding my hand, we would go down the stairs to the huge lobby below. There was a large rotating globe of the world in the lobby which displayed all of Pan Am's routes marked on it. I was too young to realize that famous people like Winston Churchill and Hollywood movie stars had flown many of those routes.

"There he is!" Mother would say again as I saw him. She would let me go so I could begin running up to him. In a playful gesture, he would place his white Pan Am uniform hat on my small head. The hat would slide down over my eyes making him disappear. The darkness never bothered me because I always knew that my father's smile was on the other side of the darkness. Even at such an early age, I knew that one day I would grow into that uniform hat and the uniform that my father wore.

Growing up in Florida, I was told stories of my great-grandfather's fishing adventures. I had no way of knowing that I would be headed into my own adventures with sailing and the world of aviation. However, one adventure would almost cost me my life. I was soon to learn what Matthew 6:34 had to say was true, "So do not worry about tomorrow; for tomorrow, will take care of itself; each day has enough trouble of its own." (NAS)

CHAPTER TWO

With a loud "BOOM!" the water rushed upwards into a hollow shaft. A shower fell from the sky lightly covering Charles Henry Price and his small sailboat. Everything became quiet as the waves subsided into ripples. The only motion breaking the placid calm was a slight ten-knot wind out of the southeast.

Below the surface of the water, a tapered silver outline floated toward the surface, breaking water near the site of the explosion...first one, then another and another.

Price was a tall, slender, sixty-year-old man in need of a shave. He straightened his overall strap, exposing the white strap mark on his left shoulder. He spat some of his chew over the side and focused his steel-blue eyes on the water. His leathery textured skin on the back of his neck wrinkled deeply as he turned his head to the left. Grabbing a long pole, he began scooping up the day's catch into the basket at the end of the pole. Even after the basket was filled twice, his prize catch still surrounded the open wooden-planked 16-foot sailboat.

It had been a long eight-hour sail the day before while tacking against the wind from Coconut Grove to the desolate Cutler area just off the Florida Keys, but the catch had been worth it.

In his usual routine, he had gathered mud from around the roots of the mangrove at the edge of the bay before beginning his journey. The sticks of dynamite were cut into quarters then packed with mud. Once the mud dried around the shortened sticks, it supplied enough weight to sink the dynamite underwater before exploding with its short fuse. The dynamite, coated with dried mud, was placed in a bucket near the transom of the boat so that he could steer and have it handy when needy.

He picked up another stick of dynamite, lighting its fuse. He tossed it in the opposite direction of the first one. As it sank to the bottom of the shallow bay area, "BOOM!" another explosion littered the surface with fish.

Again, Price scooped the surface with his long-pole bucket, filling his sailboat with fish for his return trip home.

The wind was favorable from the starboard quarter. He stashed his pole and makeshift bucket in its place under the seat alongside the centerboard well. He believed in keeping everything in its place in the small boat so that lines would not be tangled and decisions concerning sails, rigging, and his own skills of seamanship could be made with the least amount of effort. He hoisted the gaff-rigged cotton sail, mildew-stained from months of rolled up dampness, and tied the halyard off at the mast step to a two-by-four wood cleat cut and milled from Dade County Pine. He had installed the cleat when he built the boat.

The wind started filling the sail. The boat slowly began to swing downwind. Ripples followed the stern around the rudder as he set a course northward following the mangrove shoreline that would lead him back home.

Suddenly, the water was alive with the silver flashes of Mullet leaping ahead of a larger fish that was chasing after a meal. He let go of the tiller, as he reached for the halyard to lower the sail at the same time he reached for another stick of dynamite. The sail slid down the mast with enough of it remaining to cause the boat to turn into the wind. He lit the stick of dynamite and pulled his arm back to throw. Suddenly, a porpoise leaped out of the water to starboard not six feet from the red, rusty, nail-stained streaks of the side o the hull.

"Damn!" exclaimed Price in surprise and shock. Instinctively, he shifted his weight to his right leg and turned to throw the dynamite on the port side away from the porpoise. The resulting explosion deafened his ears and brought a sharp pain to his right hand.

A feeling of panic swept over him as his heart raced. He knew he had to stay awake and not fall unconscious. Within seconds, he found his world again. He had to stay under control. The nearest settlement where there may be help was more than twenty miles away.

He pulled a rag from his left back pocket and wrapped it around his forearm using his left hand and his teeth to tie a knot. The bleeding slowed down, but the knot worked loose. Blood gushed out again. He tightened the rag again, as best possible. He leaned against the tiller. The tiller began to move turning the boat into the wind. The partially raised flapping of the cotton sail sounded its chant encouraging him to crawl toward the mast and use the halyard to raise the sail all the way up.

With his teeth and one good arm, he pulled on the halyard, one foot at a time, looking up at the sail until it reached the top of the mast. The end of the halyard was wrapped around the wooden cleat and secured with a half hitch.

Price crawled back through the dead fish and his own blood that stained the bilge toward the stern. He leaned against the tiller turning the boat away from the wind. The wind filled the sail as he held the boat on an erratic northerly heading toward home. His eyes focused on the shape of the boat's ribs and the bolts that streaked rust toward the catch that lay motionless in the bilge surrounded by his own blood. He felt the weakness of the last fish that he had watched fighting for its life. He remembered that fish giving up as it tried to stay alive. The fish had flapped its tail one last time drawing in one last gasp of air that killed him.

Lying in the pile of dead fish and blood, he remembered that crisp January day with its clear blue South Florida sky. That was the day when he started placing the planks in place on the boat's frame. It was in his back yard at 2756 Day Avenue in Coconut Grove. He remembered the scent of fried chicken filling the backyard, cooked by his friend Margret "Maggie" Perdoma who came to visit and help around the house. He remembered the large tubs, next to the boat's frame, that were used every Tuesday to wash cloths next to the wringer washing machine. When tomato season was almost over, the tubs would be used to boil tomatoes and the season's canning would begin. The tomato paste would be poured into clear glass Ball jars where the tasty dark red of the stewed tomatoes would show through the glass. The jars would then be lined up in neat rows on wooden shelves in a nearby neatly organized shed until it was filled.

It was becoming more difficult to focus on the boat's details. He remembered how he had built the storage shed of milled pine. He cut down the trees after constructing a belt driven mill with parts found locally. He could still hear the steady resounding hammering of the corrugated tin as it was nailed to the two-by-four wood-framed door. That resounding sound now pounded in his head as he sat in pain.

In the heat and anxiety, the boat swerved from port to starboard and then back again, the minutes turned into hours. Charles Henry Price felt his eyes getting heavy. He saw the red of tomato season remembering the red water pouring from the large tubs. The tomato skins and remains soaked into the sandy soil of the backyard and seemed to fill the cloth he held around his hand and arm.

The hammering noise now sounded somewhere in the distance. The view of his catch in the bilge, in the rust stained ribs of the boat, the sail and large expanse of open water around him, the burning heat from the sun on his skin, all came together as he felt the boat swirling out from under him.

The unguided boat blown by the wind, left a trail of eddies as its unsteady path, from left to right, began over again. He lay against the transom sliding down into the bilge. The dead fish and his own blood became one as he lost consciousness.

The wind and boat were his only world. They were his cradle of protection. They were no longer his challenge, but his destination. He was found in his damaged boat by another fisherman. The stench of dead fish, with Charles Henry Price lying dead in his own blood, had attracted shoreline buzzards circling overhead. They became the marker that would lead to his discovery.

The plight of Charles Henry Price was the beginning of stranger things to come.

CHAPTER THREE

"No dynamite fishing for me!" but it seemed like I would carry on the family tradition of sailing. What better way to carry on that tradition than to go sailing during small-craft warnings?

The small fourteen-foot sailboat tipped low on her side as I climbed into the boat from the shallow waters where she was moored. The weather forecast was for wind gusts of thirty miles an hour. It seemed like the perfect day for a fourteen-year-old teenager eager to try out his sailing skills.

Sitting in the boat, I took the sail out of the blue waterproof bag I had wading to the boat. Both ends of the sail foot were attached to the boom as I grabbed the side of the boat holding on from a sudden wind gust. The boat, still moored, turned 180 degrees into the wind.

Crawling forward, I raised the sail as it beat a pounding rhythm against the mast while strong winds caused the boat to sway. Releasing the mooring line, the boat heeled hard over on her side as wind filled the sail. I climbed up on the high side of the hull to keep her from capsizing. A spray of salt water flew into the air as the hull cut through the waves. It was as if the hull was lashing into each wave with a vengeance.

The barrier islands, surrounding the mooring area, were disappearing into the distance. As I sailed into open water, the high waves of Biscayne Bay presented a welcome challenge. I shifted my weight to the high side of the boat, to keep it from capsizing, an adrenaline rush went through me with each wind gust on the sail. Each crashing wave was my victory as I moved forward. By not fastening off the main sheet line, I was prepared to release the line to spill air from the sail should a gust become unmanageable.

The boat's speed increased. The higher winds allowed the bow to cut through the oncoming swells with even greater force. A spray of salt and foam covered the small forward deck, partially submerging it, only to break out of the water into clear air and victory. Seeing each new wave approaching the boat, I braced for impact with a playful grin.

Tilting my head back, I enjoyed the view of white sail against blue sky. Adjusting the sail, by releasing a small amount of sheet line, I allowed the boat to pick up even more speed as it raced through the large waves.

There was suddenly a feeling of calm and ease. It was a feeling of having mastered the natural elements surrounding the boat. The boat continued slicing through the oncoming waves and plowing through the bigger ones. I laughed at the challenge that Mother Nature had sent today. Pride in my skill and mastery over nature in a fourteen-foot open sailboat with thirty mile-an-hour gusty winds felt overwhelming. Sailing didn't get much better than this. "Pride goes before destruction, and a haughty spirit before a fall" Proverbs 16:18 (NIV).

"BAM!" Suddenly the boat turned into the wind. The sail was luffing, popping like it was being torn apart by the gusty wind. It sounded like a flag trying to break free, beating itself against a flagpole. The loss of rudder control had the boat broadsided by the waves one moment and turning away from them the next. There was no way to steer. The boat was out of control.

Looking over the transom, I saw the top rudder pin had snapped in half. Disaster.

I had to do something, fast. Reaching over the transom, I tried to hold the rudder in place. The wind and waves snapped the rudder from my hand. A helpless feeling came over me. My chest felt tight. Looking over the vast open water, I couldn't see any boat nearby. Perhaps the small craft warning had kept them ashore where I should have stayed.

The boat drifted wildly in the waves and wind. Suddenly, I realized I had an even larger problem. The outgoing tide, wind, and waves were taking the boat and me with it out into the waters of the Gulf Stream. The direction of travel would take me out into the ocean after passing under the Crandon Park Bridge.

It seemed like only seconds before the bridge rushed toward the wooden fourteen-foot hull. My trembling hands held on to the side of the boat waiting for the coming crash.

The sound of a hard thump followed by the grinding sound of barnacles against wood gave me only a momentary reprieve before things became close to hopeless. It was as if everything was happening in slow motion. There was nothing that I could do to save myself. I saw myself drowning any moment among the barnacle pilings and pieces of the broken sailboat while being swept out to sea by the wind and swift outgoing tide. Immediately, I was in Charles Henry's surroundings. I imagined red blood filling the bilge as water flooded the hull. There was the stench of dead fish. My chest tightened. My throat closed as I prepared for my death.

Dropping to my knees, I tried to stabilize the flooded, unstable boat. Water continued flowing over the low side of the boat. All I could do was pray...to call out to God.

"God, I promise to never miss another day of church! Please save me!" It may have seemed like a silly prayer, but that's what I thought would make God come to my rescue.

My prayer became louder as the sound from my own voice changed into an unrecognizable high-pitched scream of panic.

"God please save me! I promise to never miss another day of church!"

The unstable swamped boat was becoming submerged, blending into the surrounding water.

"God, please save me!" came the whisper from mental fatigue as I trembled knowing death would come within minutes.

It seemed hopelessly obvious that God was preoccupied with something more important than a prideful, stupid, pleading teenager in a small, battered, sinking boat.

Looking up from the swamped bilge toward the edge of the bridge and endless open sky, I was shocked at what I saw.

There was help above me. On the bridge, I saw a young man who appeared to be in his twenties. He was wearing a white T-shirt and blue jeans. The weight of the water-filled boat was probably too heavy for a rescue, especially with the wind and tide working against him, but I needed to be rescued fast.

"Grab the mast! Pull the boat! Pull the boat to shore!" I hollered. He continued to look down at me in the sinking boat, but didn't move!

"Grab the mast! Pull the boat to shore!" He stood frozen in space as if he didn't understand what I was saying. He continued staring at my battered, sinking boat below him.

"Grab the mast!" Pull me to shore!" He learned over the side of the bridge and almost lost his balance nearly falling over the edge.

"Be careful! Grab the mast!" I repeated, screaming another hopeful plea.

Holding onto the bridge with his left hand, he reached down with his right. Extending his fingers, he touched the tip of the mast!

"Be careful! Don't give up!"

The stranger, holding on to the edge of the bridge, seemed to be gaining strength. He continued looking down at me and my situation below him. Then he spoke to me in a language that I had never heard before. It sounded like the guttural syllables of Hebrew, as I would discover later.

"Yes! Grab the mast! You almost had it! Don't give up! Pull me to safety!"

Leaning over the bridge once more, he gripped the mast more strongly. The boat started to move along the bridge toward the shore, the water becoming more shallow. The water's bottom became visible. He grabbed the mast with both hands and the boat moved quickly toward shore and the end of the bridge.

My life was saved. Elated at being alive, I jumped out of the boat into knee-deep water, I pulled the damaged hull with torn sail and broken rudder up onto the shore. Running up the rocky embankment to the top of the bridge, I was eager to thank my rescuer.

I arrived on the hot, black, asphalt road that was the top of the bridge with my heart pounding. I heard the soft sound of the wind blowing through tall Australian Pines. There were no cars or anyone. It seemed that the bridge itself had just been completed. There was no man wearing a white T-shirt and blue jeans, not even a car or bicycle. There was no sign of life. It was as if I was in the middle of a dream. Could this be real? The bridge was completely empty.

Looking down the embankment, I saw the small fourteen-foot boat, torn sail, broken rudder, half filled with water. It was real! The proof was there, but where did the stranger who saved my life go? Had God sent someone to answer my prayers?

I sat on the walkway next to the bridge railing as the sound of the wind blowing through the pines increased with a wind gust. At first, it sounded like distant thunder. Within seconds, the sound got closer. The deep mellow sound turned into a roar as its rhythm echoed off the bridge. The sound wasn't coming from around me, but from above.

Suddenly from behind the tall Australian Pines, the sky was filled with the bright yellow color of a Stearman biplane. It was beautiful. The yellow biplane had U S NAVY in black letters on the bottom of the lower wings. Round military stars were on both sides of the fuselage and out by the wing tips. The large numbers 412 were painted in black against the yellow fuselage. Red stripes were on top of the wings just inboard of the wing stars. A red stripe on the fuselage wrapped around cutting through the 412 numbers. The Stearman had a blue painted rudder. The rudder matched the blue color surrounding the military stars with their red centers.

The goggled pilot in the open cockpit reached up adjusting his cloth flying cap. He looked over the side of the open cockpit directly toward me. With his arm extended out of the cockpit, the arm of his leather flight jacket all checkered, creased, and faded, he lifted his hand to his head, fingers closed, and saluted.

The roar of the 450-horsepower radial engine and the pilot in the open cockpit soon faded again into distant thunder. Alone again with only the sound of whispering wind through the trees, everything seemed surreal. What had happened seemed unbelievable. A day of sailing ended in my near death. My life was saved by a person who did not exist. The sight and sound of the beautiful yellow biplane, with its roaring 450-horsepower radial engine fused into the sounds of those radial engines on the S-42 while I waited for my father with my mother at the Pan American seaplane terminal.

In my state of disbelief and confusion, I remembered my mother saying, "Set your mind on the things above, not on the things that are on earth" Colossians 3:2 (NAS). To a young boy of fourteen that verse could only mean one thing—airplanes were in my future.

It would be some time before I understood my mother's words. For now, I only knew one thing...I desperately had to become a pilot!

Stearman biplane like the one seen at the bridge where my sailboat crashed at Crandon Park Bridge, Miami, Florida.

CHAPTER FOUR

First flying lessons were with Charlie Burr in a Piper J-3 Cub.

There is a saying that experience is the best teacher; that experience has a greater impact on those who have experienced and have overcome obstacles and situations. Experience gives insight into a world that others may never know.

The simple maneuver of spinning an airplane is an example of those who believe that every measure and skill available should be used to avoid a spin.

On the other hand, going through the fear and uncertainty of the unknown and mastering it makes a pilot much more competent. Having the knowledge of a skill to recover from a dangerous situation means that pilot has knowledge other pilots may not have to share with their students.

The years of flying experience of Captain Chesley Burnett "Sully" Sullenberger III, known for landing the U.S. Airways Flight 1549 in the Hudson River off Manhattan, came into play when the aircraft experienced a sudden loss of power after geese were sucked into the engines. He managed to bring the plane down in the river and save the lives of 155 people on board. Sullenberger's experience had accrued from his years working as a flight instructor, an airline accident investigator, and as an F-4 military jet pilot in the Air Force.

Perhaps his most relevant experience was earning a "C" badge from the Soaring Society of America. A "C" badge is the third in a series of ABC ratings for keeping a glider in the air while flying solo for at least an hour. This task is accomplished with no engine thrust, but by using excellent judgment and evaluation of air currents lifting in hot air from the earth. The task of earning the "C" badge also requires powerless flight and landing within a relatively small distance of only 500 feet, accompanied by an instructor for verification of the accomplished task.

When pilots transition from power airplanes to gliders, one of their initial fears of powered airplane flying is the question, "What happens if the engine fails?" Every pilot needs to be ready to make emergency maneuvers if an engine fails. The procedure for engine failure is to lower the nose to gain enough airspeed to remain in the air while realizing the plane has now become a glider. The next important decision is to determine where to land, assuming there is a place to land safely. This is practical knowledge that can only be obtained and learned through experience.

Charlie Burr was not a Certified Flight Instructor. He was a gentle man and a great role model for a fourteen-year-old. I marveled at the old airplanes that always surrounded him. One of those planes was a yellow Piper J-3 Cub. With his friend, a fellow crop duster by the name of Andy Brown, he would lean against the wing of his Stearman and talk about, "When pilots were pilots; and their planes were glad!"

Charlie Burr looked at most things as learning opportunities. One such opportunity arose on a hot August afternoon. The small thermometer in the hangar read 96 degrees. Thunderstorms rolled in from the west over the Florida Everglades. Ominous dark clouds shot shafts of blinding lightening through the sky illuminating us as we stood under the roof of the open hangar. Deafening rain pounded on the hangar's tin roof. The heavy rain and thunder made it difficult to hear ourselves talk. Water started flooding the hangar floor. We watched as the water surrounded the tires of the yellow J-3 sitting in the middle of the hangar.

"Looks like a clear up!" Mr. Burr yelled to me above the pounding rain.

"Clear up?" I asked in surprise.

He smiled looking down at the flooded hangar floor. Then he looked up again toward me, raised his hand, and with closed fingers placed his hand just below his chin.

"Clear up to here!" he replied in a matter of fact manner.

The sound of the pounding rain subsided. The lightening and towering cumulus clouds moved away from the grass landing strip and made their way toward the east coast and Biscayne Bay.

"Want to go flying?" Before I could answer, he began giving me instructions.

"You sit in the backseat of the Cub. That is where the pilot sits. I'll sit in the front." Before I could say "Great!" we were pushing the Cub out of the open hangar.

Climbing into the backseat, I fastened my seatbelt. Mr. Burr walked to the front of the plane. He ran his finger tips lightly over the edge of the propeller as if addressing a trusted old friend.

"I'll call to you what I want you to do. After you do it, repeat what you did back to me."

"Okay," came my reply not sure of what was coming next.

"Switch off!"

"Switch off!" I replied after flipping the magneto switches to the off position.

"Brakes set."

"Brakes set," I repeated.

Mr. Burr pulled on the propeller trying to move the plane forward to make sure that my heels were holding the brakes firmly. Then he pulled the propeller through two cycles to prime the engine and find a compression stroke.

"Switch on!"

"Switch on!"

"Brakes set!"

"Brakes set!"

"Throttle cracked open."

"Throttle cracked open," I repeated each of his commands.

It sounded like I knew what was going on as I repeated his commands. He pulled the propeller, stepped back, and the 65-horsepower Continental engine roared to life.

Wind from the propeller filled the cockpit as I sat in the backseat of the tandem configuration of the Cub. He walked around to the folded down side door of the cockpit, climbed in, fastened his seatbelt and I expected to hear him say, "Release the brakes! My airplane!" Instead, what I heard from Charlie Burr was, "Your airplane!"

"How do I fly it?" I asked.

"Just give it what it needs" came my first bit of instruction on how to fly an airplane.

Cautiously, I moved my heels away from the two small pieces of metal on the floor that were the Cub's brakes. Adding a small amount of power, I felt the plane start to roll forward over the short freshly cut grass. Taxiing toward the short grass strip that was the runway, we moved slowly through some small puddles of standing water.

"I've got the plane!" Mr. Burr said as he moved the control stick in a circle indicating that, indeed, he was in charge. "See that orange wind sock? The wind is straight down the runway. Always take off and land into the wind. Follow me through on the controls."

"Okay" I replied, gently touching the controls while trying not to get in the way.

Full power was added. The Cub picked up speed splashing through a few small puddles. The orange wind sock and hangar raced by the open door of the plane as we majestically, though slowly, lifted into the air.

In a strange way, life itself seemed strange in the cockpit. The aroma of fresh cut grass gave way to the smell of fresh clean air cleansed by the passing storm. The wind rushed through the open door and window filling the cockpit with excitement.

The blue South Florida sky and bright sunlight flooded around the yellow J-3 Cub. Tall, billowing white clouds could be seen along the coast. We climbed for more altitude leveling off at 2,000 feet.

"Go ahead and fly it" came the voice from the front seat.

"What do I need to do?"

"Just give it what it needs," Charlie Burr replied, turning around toward his student in the backseat and offering only a smile. He knew that simple statement "Just give it what it needs" was the secret to successfully flying an airplane.

Pushing gently on the right rudder pedal and slightly moving the control stick, I put the Cub into a gentle right turn. The plane was flying under my control. It was amazing.

The green and brown farm fields of Homestead, Florida slowly moved below. "Do you like tomatoes?" came the strange question from the front seat.

What do tomatoes have to do with flying an airplane? I thought. Shouting back through the engine and wind noise, I gave a neutral answer, "Sure, I guess so!"

"I've got the plane!" he shouted as the control stick left my hand moving in a circle. Power was reduced to idle. A gentle descending turn brought us in line with an open farm field. The ground slowly rose toward the Cub. Green tomato plants, laced with red ripe tomatoes, raced past the open door of the Cub. A gentle turn to the left lined us up with two lines of bare soil that were tracts used by a tractor! Within seconds, we were sitting in the middle of a tomato field in an airplane. The little 65-horsepower engine clicked over at idle.

"This is my friend's tomato field. Jump out and pick a few tomatoes for your mom!"

Unfastening my seat belt, I got out as instructed. After picking a few tomatoes and bringing them back to the plane, I placed them in the Cub's small baggage compartment behind the backseat. We were ready to take off again.

Cargo in place! Seatbelt fastened! With power added, the Cub raced past the tomato plants with the aroma of the tomato plants filling the cockpit.

It would be many years later that I would come to understand what Charlie Burr had tried to teach by landing his J3 Cub in the middle of a tomato field.

Once again, the farm fields slowly moved below as we leveled off at 1,500 feet. "Do you like cabbage?"

"Sure" came my reply, knowing what he intended to do.

After landing at the cabbage field, I placed two cabbages in the baggage compartment with the tomatoes. Power was added and we raced along another set of tractor tracks once again gently lifting into the Florida sky.

Looking down at "Burr's International," the affectionate name given to the short grass runway surrounded by tall trees, we leveled off at 1,500 feet.

"Have you ever flown a glider?" Charlie Burr asked.

"Nope, never have."

"Would you like to fly one?"

"Sure" came my uncertain reply.

He reached over our heads with his left hand and flipped both the magneto switches to "off." Raising the nose of the plane until the relative wind could no longer turn the propeller, the propeller froze in space.

It seemed surreal. The Cub just floated silently through the air. Several Florida buzzards flew by to find out if we had discovered any updrafts of lift that they might not have noticed.

Mr. Burr checked that the Cub was trimmed for level flight. He raised his hands away from the controls putting them over his head for me to see.

"Your airplane!"

"You want me to fly?"

"If you want to."

"My airplane!" came my reply moving the controls stick left and right to acknowledge my control of the plane just like a real pilot.

"Keep your approach high until you are sure you can make the field. A gentle slip will get rid of any excess altitude and help you control your airspeed for a perfect landing."

"You want me to land it?"

"Why not? I'll talk you through it."

The orange wind sock was still straight down the runway. The Cub silently came in over the tall pine trees.

"Don't let it touch the ground," came the instructions as I listened intensely. "Don't pull the stick back so that the ground goes away, but don't let it touch the ground."

Using a slight amount of back pressure on the control stick, miraculously the wheels gently touched the grass.

"Hold the stick all the way back in your lap to keep the tail wheel on the ground for steering. Steer it just like when you taxied."

We rolled down the runway in silence. A small amount of right rudder turned the plane toward the gas pump located just off the runway. We rolled to a stop, unfastened our seatbelts and climbed out of the plane as though it was a normal day of flying.

A few weeks after we had flown, my father and uncle Charles Price were working with Charlie Burr at something that seemed very unusual. They were cutting down large Florida holly trees that were growing wild. The trees filled the space between the ground and the telephone wires that they were under.

On the other side of the wires from where they were working was a small one-acre farm field planted with beans. The leaves of the bean plants had been shredded by the insects. Telephone wires were at one end of the field and tall pine trees on the opposite end.

The owner of the infected bean field was a friend of Charlie Burr. His friend's spray equipment had broken down so he was at the mercy of nature and the insects.

My father and uncle continued chopping away at the massive holly trees, clearing a path under the wires. After the space was cleared, Charlie Burr borrowed another friend's open cockpit Stearman biplane. Loading the 60-gallon aluminum spray tank in the front cockpit, once used to carry passengers, Charlie climbed into the aft cockpit, adjusted his flying goggles that were attached to the cloth cap he had placed over his head. The large radial engine belched out two puffs of white smoke as the propeller started to turn. The 450-horsepower engine roared to life. The plane raced down Burr's small, short airstrip toward the nearby bean field. The plane screamed in a dive while lining up with the field as it passed under the telephone wires and the space that had been cleared. Immediately after passing under the wires, the tall green pine trees filled the view from the cockpit as the plane raced toward them.

As he pulled the biplane up almost vertically over the pines, the dark green of the trees was replaced by the clear blue sky. The wind beat into the cockpit as the plane dove down over the pines while lining up for his final pass with spray turned on. The trail of spray was left spinning behind the turbulence from the plane's wingtips. My father and uncle stood under the cleared space below the wires, moving out of the way as Charlie Burr once more made his final pass under the wires. He departed the small bean field, making a steep climb, then landing back at his own airstrip.

CHAPTER FIVE

Pitts Special 150 horsepower with a new paint job. It cannot be seen, but "Tiny Dancer" appears in front of the windshield, named from the lyrics of Elton John's song of the same name. The Pitts Special made an emergency landing in a field. Aerobatic Pitts Special "Tiny Dancer" is a wonderful airplane capable of doing many aerobatics with its biplane wings, external wing and tail braces, and small lifting surfaces.

It would be many flights in the future before the experience of that first flight with Charlie Burr would become applicable.

The small, single-seat red and white Pitts Special aerobatic biplane was equipped with 150 horsepower. The name "Tiny Dancer" from Elton John's song of the same title was printed in white on the fuselage in front of the cockpit.

The student I had just flown with in my Citabria said that he had never seen a Pitts Special fly. That was all the encouragement I needed

Opening the fuel cap in front of the windshield, I checked the fuel in the dim hangar light. The plastic fuel sight gauge was a tube extending below the fuel tank inside of the cockpit. The gauge indicated that there was plenty of fuel for my short aerobatic demonstration flight. Since the Pitts was an S1C and single place, my student would have to watch the aerobatics from the ground.

The deep red paint job sparkled in the sunlight as I pushed the small Pitts out of the hangar. Climbing into the cockpit, I fastened the seatbelt, adjusted the parachute, and gave a final tug on the shoulder harness. The engine roared to life.

After we lined up with the runway, our rapid acceleration made the hangar race by as back pressure on the control stick brought the plane into an almost vertical climb.

The altimeter read 3,000 feet. My airshow was ready to begin. A loop pushed me deep into the bottom of the seat as the earth-colored farm fields below morphed into the blue sky filling the windshield. The engine screamed down the back side of the loop, into view patterns of farm fields below, coming quickly.

The airspeed entry read 120 MPH, as the nose lifted slightly above the horizon. I moved the stick and rudder left. The earth and sky rolled in front of the Pitts as they seemed to fold into each other.

With my eyes squinting into the sun, I lowered the nose for the Pitts to gain speed to 140 MPH. Pulling the control stick back into a tight loop inverted at the top, I started a slight forward pressure that sent the plane in an inverted 45 degree down line ending with a half roll to right-side-up flight. That maneuver completed one half of a Cuban Eight.

In a vertical reverse maneuver, I added full power into a climb! At the top of the climb, the plane almost stopped. Then I added full left rudder that returned the plane to a perfect vertical dive. The ground raced up toward the small aerobatic Pitts Special biplane. The plane returned to level flight. With the airport in sight, I leveled off at 1,000 feet and turned toward the airport. Suddenly, the healthy roar of the Pitt's 150 horse power engine became silent.

The fuel gauge under the tank showed that fuel was still available. Electrical switches were still "on" and everything looked in order. To verify that the fuel tank was not empty, I rocked the wings to scavenge any remaining fuel should this be the case. Rocking the wings, the engine roared to life. Then the engine became silent as fast as it had started, apparently as the last drops of fuel were burned.

The Pitts Special biplane is a wonderful airplane capable of doing many things. With biplane wings, external wing and tail braces, and small lifting surfaces, gliding is not one of those wonderful things.

The airport was in sight, but out of gliding range. With an altitude of 1,000 feet, the Pitts started sinking fast. Below I saw a clear smooth-looking farm field. I made a steep 180-degree turn and had the Pitts lined up with the field into the wind for a landing.

"Ever fly a glider?" came Charlie Burr's words. "Keep the approach high until you are sure you can make the field. A gentle slip will dissipate altitude and help you control airspeed for a perfect landing."

Lined up with the farm field, I made a small amount of left stick and right rudder that sent the Pitts into a slip. Altitude disappeared fast. Small tomato plants began to pass by. I lined up with two dirt tracks made by tractor tires. Fearing that the Pitts might flip over in soft soil, I reached up sliding the bubble canopy all the way aft for a quick exit out of the open cockpit. Outside air rushed into the cockpit along with the familiar smell of tomato plants.

"Take some home for your Mom!" I remember Charlie Burr once telling me.

The wheels of the Pitts gently kissed the firm soil of the tractor tracks rolling a short distance before stopping. Before I could unbuckle my parachute, shoulder harness, and seatbelt, my student, who had watched it all, came running across the field through the tomato plants.

We lifted the tail of the lightweight Pitts into the bed of my Ford Ranger truck. The tail wheel of the plane rested on the lowered tail gate. Sheepishly, I towed the Pitts out of the field. There was no crop damage. I towed the plane down the paved road to Richard's Field. Stopping at the fuel pump, I refueled the Pitts and towed it back into the hangar.

It was a lesson well learned. A fun flight in a J-3 Cub with Charlie Burr had a purpose that only he knew too well. That purpose was not only to save my life, but to learn how to teach others to simply "fly the plane" by giving it what it needs.

Indeed, "Continue in the things you have learned and become convinced of knowing from whom you have learned them" (2 Timothy 3:14).

This Pitts Special flight was to happen in the future. For now, it was time to fly with a Certified Flight Instructor. It was time to buy a Pilot Log Book and start logging flight time so that I could solo an airplane. It was also time to learn that all flight instructors are not equal. Instead of the calm, laid-back style of Charlie Burr, I was about to step into the world of instruction from a World War II P-51 ace fighter pilot.

Chapter Six

On top of Jim Lowry's desk, there was a black baseball cap that looked new. The front of the cap had two connected, pure white, angel wings. In the center of the wings, a red shield had a small white airplane outline as viewed from above. Under the plane was a gray banner with the words "EARN YOUR WINGS" embroidered in black.

Jim Lowry leaned against his dark mahogany desk, wearing a military leather flight jacket which he'd worn during World War II. His job had been to destroy the enemy using his flying skills. His weapon was a P-51 Mustang.

His arms were folded across his chest as I walked into the room. He was guarding his own personal space. The top of his desk was littered with aviation magazines as well as a Miami Sectional Chart. The chart had red lines drawn over its yellow and blue features on a background of light green. The red lines formed a triangle connecting one airport to another. Speaking with a raspy voice, he kept his head low, making it difficult to listen to him. His eyes looked up intensely from his lowered head much like a parent ready to scold his child. His short military salt and pepper hair was snow white just above his ears.

"So, you want to clean planes? We can always use someone to clean those planes" were Lowry's first words to me. He looked down as if talking to the floor in his flat Chicago accent, he continued, "You'll be paid eight dollars per hour. You can exchange each eight dollars for one hour of flight time."

He moved his hands through the air in front of him when he spoke, turned them up and toward me as if inquiring of my acceptance or rejection of his proposal.

"That sounds great! I really want to learn how to fly."

"Good to hear that," Lowry replied picking up the Miami Sectional Chart off the top of his desk after moving some of the aviation magazine clutter out of the way.

"See this chart with the red lines drawn in the red ink?"

"Yes sir."

"Well, you don't do something stupid like that!"

"No sir," I replied having no idea what he was talking about.

"When you fly at night the red lines disappear due to the red cockpit lights. I had to chew ass because this student lost those red True Course lines in the red cockpit light. Can you remember that."

"Yes sir. I will remember not to make red lines," came my unsteady reply.

Lowry carried himself with confidence. It showed as he walked away from his desk. It was a sort of swagger developed from flying combat missions over Germany. He had become an ACE by shooting down 250 enemy planes.

Twice he had to use his parachute, bailing out when his plane was on fire with flames licking into the cockpit.

He placed the Sectional Chart back on his desk, folded his arms back over his chest, lowered his head as he looked at me. Unfolding his arms, without saying a word, he pointed to the door. The interview was over. He put his hands deep into his pants pockets and nodded his approval.

The early morning sunlight illuminated the shapes and colors of airplanes. Walking the path beside the corrugated tin hangar toward Lowry's office, I took a deep breath. The fresh, cool, morning air felt like a new beginning. Noticing every detail of my surroundings, I saw small pink and white wild flowers growing between the stepping stones next to the hangar. Life seemed so simple, a small flower growing next to a hangar containing magnificent flying machines.

Lowry was standing next to the open door of the flight school's office.

"You are almost late here!" came his morning greeting.

Looking at my watch, I saw that I was a half-hour early. Lowry wasn't about to cut me any slack. My father's words entered my thoughts, "Children should be seen and not heard!" My father's words reinforced the fact that a reply was not necessary. In a strange way, I knew that Lowry would stand up to any challenge. Especially if that challenge would jeopardize the safety of his students. My senses were heightened as we walked toward the small Aeronca 7AC Champ. The 7AC Champion Aircraft had dirty white paint with a dull green stripe painted down the side of the fuselage. I would be sharing my first official hour of dual flight instruction with an actual P-51 fighter pilot.

As I held the brakes for Lowry, he pulled the propeller through and the engine roared to life. Wind from the propeller blast and the smell of burned fuel flooded into the cockpit through the Champ's open window. We were going to fly.

Arriving at the run up area, we went through the check list:

"Flight controls free and clear."

"Fuel selector on."

"Engine run up, oil pressure in the green."

"Magneto check drop 75 RPM each magneto."

"Carburetor Heat drop checked."

We lined the plane up facing the Control Tower waiting for clearance to take off. Out of the dark tinted control tower window, I saw the bright steady green light signal. We were cleared for takeoff.

Moving the control stick in a circle indicating that we had received the "steady green" to the tower, we lined up on the runway for takeoff. The plane slowly began to move. Lowry applied full power. The runway lights began to race by the side of the plane.

"You've got the plane!" Lowry shouted above the engine noise.

"What do you want me to do?"

"Fly the damn airplane!"

Grabbing the controls of the plane under pressure, I immediately started turning left toward the side of the paved runway. We were out of control.

"Keep the damn thing straight! Did you forget how to use your feet? Use your damn feet on the rudder peddles!"

Just as we had shot off to the left side of the runway, we used too much right rudder and the plane shot off to the right toward the impending runway lights. My heart pounded, my muscles tightened as Lowry began shouting more instructions.

"Keep the damn thing straight. Push the stick forward."

The tail rose into the air, but we were still headed toward the edge of the runway.

"What the hell are you waiting for? Pull the damn stick back and let's fly."

Slowly pulling back on the control stick, I watched as the edge of the pavement and runway lights passed under the plane.

"Reduce to climb power. Reduce 100 rpms to climb power now."

It was as if the instructor was still flying his WWII 2,270 horsepower Rolls Royce P-51 Mustang. Reducing the little struggling 65 horsepower Continental by 100 rpm to climb power, I brought the Aeronca Champ under control as it lumbered slowly into the air, struggling to gain altitude.

To the west, I leveled off at 3,000 feet. I felt the control stick move out of my hand in a circle to let me know that Lowry was flying the plane.

"I've got the plane!" came his command shouted from the rear seat. Lowry added full power and the plane went almost vertical as he pulled back on the control stick. Every muscle in my body tightened as I hung on to the seat cushion with both hands not knowing what to expect. Just as quickly as we began the climb, the nose of the plane dropped. The wild roller coaster ride continued pushing me out of the seat, straining me against my seat belt, and then returning to level flight.

"That there was a power on stall. You need to do the next one in order not to be afraid should it ever happen to you."

Not to be afraid? He must be kidding.

"Okay, here we go," came my uncertain reply.

Full power, nose up, the ground vanished from the windshield and blue sky appeared. Suddenly, the left wing dropped. We were in a downward spiral with full power to the left. Airspeed increased rapidly as we raced toward the ground. The controls were slapped out of my hands. Lowry recovered from the maneuver using the dual controls in the backseat.

"Rudder to keep it straight. Power off when things get out of control. Now try it again."

Try it again? I thought with my body shaking from nerves.

Strangely, the next attempt was successful. The nose of the plane recovered straight ahead to straight and level flight.

The controls were once again slapped out of my hands, "My airplane. You need to watch this," Lowery said siting behind me.

The control stick was pulled all the way back into our laps. Power was reduced to idle. Just as the "Champ" stalled, Lowery applied full left rudder still holding the stick firmly in his lap. The earth below changed into spinning colors in a blur of motion. Lowry applied full right rudder, forward control stick, and the earth suddenly stood still as if nothing had ever happened.

"That was a one turn spin. You need to give it a try for yourself.

"You want me to do that?"

"Isn't that what I just said?"

"Yes sir."

Gently pulling the control stick back into my lap, I waited for the cyclone to begin. My legs were shaking as the power off climb ended in a stall.

"Hold the stick back. Don't let go. Full left rudder now," came more commands.

Doing as instructed by Lowry, I let the plane drop off into a spin.

"Three quarters around. Push right rudder now," came the orders shouted from behind my head.

The cyclone stopped. The plane was in straight and level flight. It was amazing. For the first time flying with Lowry, I felt in control of the airplane.

"Can we do another one?"

"Wouldn't have it any other way," came the reassuring voice from the backseat. "Give me one more and then we will head back toward the airport."

On the downwind leg of the traffic pattern, Tamiami Tower flashed the green light giving us permission to continue our approach. On final approach, Lowry took the controls. We received a steady green from the tower that cleared us to land.

"I've made a few more landings on pavement than you have, so I'll make this one," Lowry announced.

The tires chirped on the pavement, signaling an end to my first hour of "official" dual flight training.

The next five hours of dual instruction would be flying around the edge of a cow pasture, making S-turns along a road, more stalls, spins, and finally landings and take offs.

It was during the sixth lesson that Lowry sat in the backseat of the Champ. He had not said a word during my last three landings. Suddenly, he spoke.

"You are as good as you are going to get. Stop and let me out."

Applying a slight amount of brakes, we made the first turn off onto the taxiway after landing.

"Remember the damn cross wind from the left. Keep the damn left wing down. I don't want to be picking up airplane pieces and body parts." came Lowry's last words of encouragement as he deplaned from the Champ. He found a spot and stood on the taxiway next to the runway.

Lining up on the runway, with a bright steady green light from the tower, I was cleared for takeoff.

Applying just enough rudder to keep it straight, forward pressure on the control stick, lifting the tail, and with a slight amount of back pressure, I got the plane to gently lift into the sky. I looked out of the side window and there was my flight instructor, the P-51 fighter pilot. He was standing, looking at the ground, with his arms folded. When the plane flew by, he looked up, unfolded his arms, hooked his left thumb in his pants pocket, and raised his right hand into a "thumbs up" showing his confidence and approval.

"Remember that you have a left cross wind so keep the left wing down when you land" echoed in my mind. There would be no airplane pieces and body parts on my watch.

Airspeed and altitude looked good. As I came in to the final approach, the steady green from the tower cleared me to land once more. The large white number 9 on the threshold of the runway slowly moved up toward the belly of the Champ as I passed over it.

"Keep the left wing down" entered my thoughts as I planned a perfect landing just like my last three. The upwind left tire chirped touching the pavement first. It was a perfect landing.

Suddenly, the right wing lifted. The plane was back into the air. Rubber began squealing against the runway asphalt when the plane touched down again. With a feeling of horror in the pit of my stomach, the plane was sliding across the pavement toward the runway lights and the left side of the runway.

"Oh shit! Lowry is going to kill me! Airplane pieces and body parts," came into my thoughts within seconds.

Then other thoughts entered my mind from my first flight with Charlie Burr, "Just give it what it needs." Then strangely, Burr's words were reinforced by Lowry's training, "Fly the damn plane."

Right wing down to stop the drift to the left. Left rudder to keep the plane straight on the runway. Control stick gently all the way back into my lap. "PLOP!" the Champ ran out of airspeed and firmly, but safely, made its last of three bounces onto the paved runway.

My heart pounded. How could I have messed up my first solo landing so badly? He was standing on the taxiway, head down as usual, arms crossed. This time I was certain to have disappointed Lowry.

To my surprise, he raised his head, looked directly into the cockpit, held his hand up pointing to the orange windsock. The wind had changed to a crosswind coming from the right. It had not been the left cross wind as instructed, and flown, during the last three landings. Lowry raised his hand over his head making a circling motion for me to continue for another solo try. Then something I never expected. Lowry gave me a thumbs-up showing his approval.

With the fear of Lowry's disapproval gone, I seemed to feel a different connection to life. Something impossible to explain. A steady green light shone again. Once again. I was racing down the runway. It was as if that steady green light from the tower had approved of me as a pilot.

The Champ raced down the runway past Lowry once more. He stood with his right hand in the air for another thumbs-up. Then he put both hands deep into his pants pockets, looked down at the ground and swaggered away from the active runway as if to say his job had been successfully completed.

It has been said that we are born alone and that we shall die alone. In that moment, racing down the runway, with the sweet sound of a 65-horsepower Continental filling the cockpit, with just enough rudder to keep the plane straight, using a slight amount of back pressure on the stick, and lifting the plane into the sky, I felt as though I had been born again. I was a pilot.

Tamiami Airport where I soloed would eventually become the sprawling campus of Florida International University. The runways gave way to building foundations and airport operations would eventually be moved out west to new Tamiami Airport. The phrase "FIU in '72" was the motto of all the students from Miami-Dade Community College wanting to attend Florida International University. Years later while I walked around the FIU campus, I noticed that the only remaining building of Tamiami Airport was the control tower, which had been turned into the campus security building.

After my solo, my father purchased a basket case of an airplane project. It was an Aeronca 11AC Chief. Unlike the tandem seating of the J-3 and "Champ," the Chief had side-by-side seating and a control yoke instead of the control stick. The project was placed into an open shed that we had in the backyard. Fabric was hanging off the airframe, exposing the steel tubing frame. The plane looked like it had been damaged by a hurricane.

My assignment, after my day in high school, was to pull off the rest of the fabric so that the plane could be recovered after any rust or corrosion was removed. Other jobs were assigned when my father returned home from trips with Pan Am. He was flying land planes from Miami International Airport, once called the "36th Street" Airport. Without the speed of jets, his trips would often last several weeks.

When my father returned home, I would be prepared for his lessons.

"The sign of a good mechanic is to know when to stop tightening things!" He usually said that to me after I had sheared something in half from trying to do a perfect job to impress him.

"Never allow anyone to smoke around a fabric covered airplane." he said after stuffing a 55-gallon drum with the old fabric pulled from the Chief. A match was tossed into the container! "SWOOSH!" The fabric vanished in a matter of seconds leaving the 55-gallon container completely empty.

The Aeronca Chief was finally completed. It was assembled, and test flown with the help of Charlie Burr at his grass airstrip.

It was time to prove to my father that he could be proud of my flying ability, even though my ability as a mechanic might not be quite up to speed. I would prove to him that I had superior pilot skills. After all, I had flown with a P-51 fighter pilot. I had mastered spins and was certain my father had never even done a spin.

There was another saying my father had, "A little knowledge is a dangerous thing; and you have a hell of a lot of a little knowledge." It was time for a sixteen-year-old with a Student Pilot's License to prove my father's saying was correct.

"A fool takes no pleasure in understanding, but only in expressing his opinion" Proverbs 18:12 (NIV). And even more applicable, "If you stop listening to instruction, my son, you will stray from the words of knowledge." Proverbs 19:27 (ESV).

Chapter Seven

The Aeronca Chief was designed for personal use. With its 65 horsepower, it did not have much power and was not certified for aerobatic flight.

I pushed forward on the control yoke of the Aeronca Chief, as the blue surface of Naranja Lake of Homestead, Florida, below filled the windshield. The airspeed indicator climbed from 80, to 90, then 100, and finally to 120 miles an hour. The tires of the plane were inches above the surface of the water as a skier passed by the right side of the plane. I waved.

In front of the plane was the ski-jump. The euphoria, along with a feeling of supreme confidence, was all that mattered.

The ramp became larger. With slight back pressure on the yoke, the lake and ski-jump were left far below as I climbed into the bright South Florida sky. Circling over the lake, I rocked my wings taking a bow for my performance of mastering a ski-jump with an airplane.

High over the Homestead, Florida farm fields, I leveled the plane at 4,000 feet. Next to me in the right seat were six rolls of toilet paper. It wasn't the softest brand, but a less expensive brand of toilet paper that would unroll more easily.

The outside air rushed in through the open cockpit window. The first roll was tossed through the opened window and transformed into a long white streamer.

I applied a quick forward pressure on the yoke and made a tight descending turn to the left. The toilet paper attack had begun. The long white streamer raced toward the windshield. With a slight left turn to hit the target, "poof!" the wing sliced the streamer in half.

Another turn, another slice, and another until the long streamer was in pieces. The altimeter read 1,000 feet which was my predetermined hard deck below which not to descend.

Level at 1,000 feet, flying west, I noticed a short, abandoned grass airstrip just under the plane. Power reduced and a circle overhead, I soon had the tires rolling over the tall grass.

Within what seemed like seconds, out of the tall weeds surrounding the abandoned runway, the area came alive with the U. S. Border Patrol.

Two cars pulled out onto the runway. The plane was surrounded. One car stopped in front of the plane while another car came along the pilot's side of the plane.

The driver's side door of both cars flew open as the Agents drew their guns from behind the opened doors. I shut down the engine; the propeller froze to a stop. Both Agents, with guns still drawn, cautiously walked toward the little red and white Aeronca Chief.

"What are you doing?" came the first question in an authoritative voice from the Agent now standing outside of the cockpit window. Before I could answer, there was another command from the second Agent now standing next to the first.

"Get out of the plane! Keep your hands where we can see them!" Getting out of the plane, I held both hands up into the air.

"Who were you trying to signal?"

"Nobody."

"What were you doing?"

"Just cutting toilet paper for practice."

"Let me see your license!"

The Agent looked over my Student Pilot's License. He verified that I was a citizen of the United States of America.

"We thought you might be signaling someone. Cubans have been smuggled into our country and there will soon be something called the Cuban-American Dry Foot Policy. They will be allowed to stay once they set foot on American soil. It will be a good deal for them because our government will pay them to resettle in America. Until then we are going to intercept anyone entering America illegally."

There was no way of knowing that in the future, over a one year period, 51,000 undocumented Cubans would enter our country. This was above the 20,000 Cubans given official permission annually by the United States. A little-known fact was with their entry and benefits into America they would be given permission to fly back and forth to Cuba on charter flights out of Miami International Airport. These flights were only available to Cuban nationals.

Both Agents were more relaxed as they holstered their guns and leaned against their patrol cars. The two Federal Agents seemed like nice guys. Not thinking of the restriction on my Student Pilot's License not to carry passengers, I innocently asked, "Would either of you like to go flying?"

"No thank you" came their reply at the same time. It was just as well because it would have been a violation of the

Federal Aviation Regulations for me to take up a passenger. They turned, walked back to their patrol cars, opened the doors, and drove away through the tall weeds of the abandoned airstrip.

The takeoff was uneventful. Leveling off at 1,500 feet, I was soon flying over a new housing development that would become South Miami Heights. My uncle, Chuck Price, happened to be doing construction work on the site. Below was a long stretch of dirt road in the soon to be developed housing project.

With the power reduced to idle, I made a tight low pass turn lining up with the dirt road to make sure it was suitable for landing. It looked like a good place to land, so I added full power in a climb coming around again ending in a perfect landing.

Before I could get the plane stopped, a cloud of dust pulled up along the side of the plane. In the middle of the dust was Mr. Woolem, the owner of the development, sitting inside an old pick-up truck.

"What the hell do you think you are doing!" he yelled above the nose of the plane's engine.

"Just landed to talk to my Uncle. He's Chuck Price."

"Well, I don't know how you got this damn thing in here, but I hope you can get it the hell back out!"

"No problem!" I yelled back, spinning the plane around with full power for take off. A large dust cloud formed into a cyclone around the owner's truck obscuring it from view.

After takeoff and climbing to 500 feet, I circled the building site. Seeing Uncle Chuck below, I rocked the wings to say, "Hello."

Before long, I was flying over the open farm fields of Homestead and Naranja, Florida.

A small house with a long dirt road in front of the house was recognizable. The bright yellow bikini bathing suit, worn by the young woman sunning herself on the front lawn, was the same young woman who was my prom date at South Dade High School. It was time to impress her with my piloting skills.

As I dove toward the long dirt road with full power and the little 65-horsepower engine screaming, my thoughts were preoccupied with the yellow bikini.

I could make out every detail on her beach towel as I accelerated the plane along the rural county dirt road. I flew inches above the dry road, a cloud of dust following the plane. She would be so proud of me. Roaring past, I waved out the open side window. "How great is this!" I thought as she sat up on the blanket waving back.

Thoughts of when we slow danced together and how she was wearing a Bird of Paradise wrist corsage at the South Dade High School prom flooded over me. The corsage was created from a Bird of Paradise plant my father was growing. He had a large "bird" flower business, but inexpensive imports ultimately forced him to close the business.

Staying as low as possible over the dirt road, I thought I would surely impress her. My mission had been accomplished. I smiled thinking how important I had become. Time to get back to flying the plane.

Turning my attention from the yellow bikini on the lawn to looking outside the windshield, I saw that my world of clear blue sky had turned into the dark green of tall Australian Pine trees. Uh-oh!

Pulling back slowly on the yoke and trying not to stall, I maintained full power, but the small 65-horsepower engine labored to cooperate. Momentum was lost from the highspeed pass as the plane strained to stay airborne.

Airspeed decreased. The pine trees grew taller. The plane started to mush into the top of the trees.

Slowly lowering the nose, I prayed for enough airspeed to climb over the trees. The airspeed started to increase. The height of the trees increased. Releasing a small amount of back pressure on the yoke to keep flying. I moved the plane closer to the trees. With the slight increase in airspeed, the plane continued to fly at the edge of stalling. Pine needles passed inches away from the tires. Slowly, the tops of the trees passed behind the plane. Seconds later, I had survived crashing into the trees.

Leveling off at 500 feet, I made a slight turn to see if my admirer had witnessed my close call with death. She had. She had run into the house where it was safe.

Enough low altitude flying for one day. It was time to climb for altitude where it would be impossible to get into any more trouble.

Watching the peaceful, detached, puffs of white cumulus clouds looking like enemy gun fire from an anti-aircraft gun and glancing at the altimeter, I was now flying at 4,000 feet.

Remembering the airshow at Sun-n-Fun, I thought of one maneuver that looked easy to do. The maneuver would be considered an aerobatic maneuver because it would have more than 30 degrees of pitch. The Chief was not stressed or designed for aerobatics. The plane would not be doing anything crazy like going upside down. This maneuver consisted of going straight up, and then straight down, with a turn at the top to change direction. The name of the maneuver is a Vertical Reverse or Hammerhead Turn. Straight up and straight down, I wondered how difficult could that be? I wasn't stupid enough to overstress a plane not designed to do aerobatics. No rolls or loops, just straight up and straight down. Why not?

Lowering the nose of the plane, I focused on the airspeed indicator. The speed increased to 120 miles an hour. I gently pulled back on the yoke, adding full power. The wing tip was set vertically against the outside horizon.

"How cool is this!" I thought, realizing that the airspeed was still too fast to turn for the down line. The plane came to the top of the climb with full power. It stopped climbing and was stationary as it hung in the air.

"Now!" I yelled "This is it! Time to turn!" Full left rudder. Yoke still holding the wing tip vertical.

Nothing happened. The plane slowly started falling backwards. The speed to make the turn had fallen to zero. There was not enough momentum for the plane to continue to fly.

The controls felt like they were not connected to anything. There was a complete loss of control! The plane went into a tail slide and then flipped over inverted! Once the plane was upside down, the engine was starved for fuel. It quit. Everything loose in the cockpit drifted up to the ceiling. Maps, pencils, and two oil cans from the baggage compartment looked like they were glued to the headliner.

TO LOOK UPWARD: ONE FLIGHT INSTRUCTOR'S JOURNEY

With lips and chin trembling, I was trapped in an airplane, falling inverted without an engine. I was busting my lungs in excited breathing. I almost felt a scream coming, but that would come in the last second before the crash. The plane was falling out of the sky inverted toward the ground.

There was nothing I could do, but release the controls and hang on to the seat cushion to await certain death. As if by magic, once I let go of the controls, the plane's design took over. The plane swapped ends with the nose headed toward the ground rolling right side up at the same time. Fuel flow returned to the engine as it restarted.

Holding on to the controls again in straight and level flight, I recalled my father's words: "A little knowledge is a dangerous thing; and you have a hell of a lot of little knowledge!"

There were also words that pertained to my haughty spirit, "Better is the latter of a thing than its beginning; better is the patient spirit than the haughty of spirit" Ecclesiastes 7:8 (TLT).

It was time to be thankful that my haughty spirit had survived my "hell of a lot of little knowledge!" It was also time to "Listen to advice and accept discipline and at the end you will be counted among the wise." Proverbs 19:20 (NIV).

With slightly over 200 hours of flight time as a Student Pilot trying to crash into Pine trees, drown in a lake, and being reprimanded by the United States Border Patrol, I finally realized that there might possibly be a better way to put my piloting skills to use. The Proverb that pride comes before the fall had not completely ended in my death this time. I finally realized that my father might have been on to something.

Chapter Eight

I flew a Citabria in the Homestead Airshow 800' in an inverted pass although the plane had no inverted system for fuel and oil.

It was time to see if my father's uniform hat would fit without sliding down over my eyes. It was time to follow in my father's footsteps, not as a mechanic, but as a pilot.

National Airlines, Eastern Airlines, and Pan Am all suggested that, if I wanted to be hired, I would have to log "heavy time" in airplanes weighing over 12,500 pounds.

My quest for "heavy time" motivated me to arrive at Miami International Airport at two in the morning. My entry into the world of non-schedule cargo flying had begun. My job was flying as co-pilot on both the C-46 and DC-4 aircraft.

A cold wind blew in from the North through the damp morning air and darkness. The cargo arrived in three semi-truck loads. The large cargo door on the side of the C-46 was opened and a ramp was rolled into place.

The cattle were guided up the ramp through the wide cargo door. It did not take long to discover that this was not my father's world of flying people on a scheduled basis.

From the cargo door along the floor of the fuselage up to the cockpit, cow dung stuck to the bottom of my uniform shoes like heavy, wet mud. The body heat from the animals caused the cockpit ceiling to drip water onto the seats, controls, and instruments. Beneath the fuselage, during the pre-flight, cattle urine flowed out over the internal control cables like a waterfall. The urine pounded the asphalt below like heavy rain.

The only advantage to flying cattle was that they didn't kick the inside of the fuselage like race horses or leave feathers everywhere like chickens.

On an assignment to fly telephone equipment to Lima, Peru, I left Miami for the forty-hour flight at one in the morning. We were flying over Havana, Cuba. We were in the same C-46, with patched bullet holes in the vertical stabilizer, reminders that the plane had participated in the failed Bay of Pigs invasion. In fact, the Captain flying the plane had also been flying this very C-46 during the invasion.

The invasion was launched from the United States to overthrow Dictator Fidel Castro. The United States pulled out at the last minute leaving the Cubans stranded without backup from the United States.

This morning the city lights of Havana sparkled up out of the darkness and pitch black water surrounding the city.

"If we have a complete power failure, we will not go down!" the captain exclaimed, with a slight Cuban accent, wiping the sweat off his face with a handkerchief retrieved from his back pants pocket.

We reached Panama and refueled. We were on our way to Peru, but first we had to cross the Andes Mountains. The elevation of the mountains, generally being 22,841 feet, were spread out over 4,500 miles along the western coast of South America. They are the world's largest mountain range.

In the blackness of night, over the mountains, red cockpit lights illuminated the flight instruments, but were jarred into a blur from the severe turbulence. Navigation was supplied by watching the low frequency Automatic Direction Finder

(ADF) needle spin wildly toward each lightening strike that illuminated the cockpit. With turbulence pounding the plane, the magnetic compass spun wildly leading us to a small almost abandoned airport by the name of Talara. Our approach showed a high elevation where nothing existed but a barren landscape.

Once on the ground, wearing my short sleeve cotton uniform shirt, I realized that what the books say about the Equator was correct. If you leave Miami in August, you arrive on the other side of the Equator in winter. I arrived without as much as a jacket.

After six months of flying cargo, it was time to show National, Eastern, and Pan Am my "heavy time." Each interview produced stacks of pilot applications from young pilots who were getting their experience from the military. Even more important to the airlines, these young pilots had all flown jet aircraft and would not have to be trained to fly jets.

I did not qualify to fly the airline jets, so I went back to my true love: stick-and-rudder skills and passing those skills along to others as a Certified Flight Instructor. My dream as a young child of wearing my father's uniform with his white Pan Am uniform hat was not going to happen. I knew he would be disappointed with me although he would never say a word.

Purchasing a Citabria with its tandem seating high wing and tail wheel was the perfect plane to teach pilots stick-and-rudder skills and basic aerobatics.

To promote my flight school business, I arrived at Homestead General Aviation Airport early on a Saturday morning before the crowds arrived. The event was the Aviation Expo of South Florida.

The Federal Aviation Administration gave approval for a low altitude waiver. The approval was for a low level aerobatic demonstration. The Citabria had the smaller 0-235, 115-horse power engine. There was no inverted fuel system. Once inverted, the engine would be starved for fuel causing it to go silent.

The crowd of spectators lined the east-west runway. The plane rose high above the crowd, the altimeter indicated 3,000 feet. Lowering the nose to build up speed, lining up with the runway for the inverted flying and the aerobatic sequence, I began a loop to prepare for the maneuvers.

Speakers lined the row of spectators as the announcer flooded over and through the crowd.

"Watch as Rob Mixon approaches from the left. He will attempt to do a low pass. Not just a low pass, but a low inverted pass. Not just a low pass inverted, a low pass inverted with the engine starved for fuel. An actual inverted power failure. Watch now as Rob Mixon approaches from your left and the Citabria, aerobatic spelled backwards, rolls into the inverted position!"

The roar of the engine popped its last breath with a flash of sunlight on the leading edge of the wing bringing the

Citabria to the inverted position. Only seconds ago, the sound of an airplane screaming for airspeed, now turned into the whisper of wind. The Citabria silently passed inverted flying at an altitude of only 800 feet near the crowd of spectators.

I passed the crowd, rolling to right-side-up, keeping a farm field in sight if the engine could not come back to life. The maneuver was successful. The sound of the engine roared once again through the crowd and my part of the airshow had ended.

Three weeks had passed since the Homestead Airshow, Homestead, Florida. The demonstration had brought in students who were soloing in six hours. At the same time, many were accomplishing all the aerobatic maneuvers the Citabria was certified to do. All of this on only a Student Pilot License.

The Citabria was paying the bills, but after the bills were paid, it was time to pay for maintenance, fuel, insurance, or hangar rent. A new flight school named Burnside-Ott Aviation Training Center was opening at New Tamiami Airport.

Burnside-Ott was bringing in new Cessna 150s in flights of ten direct from the factory. The pay was eight dollars an hour per flight. Every time a student flew solo, the Pilot Instructor would receive fifty cents. We could get paid even during our days off. Within a short time of flight instructing, I bought for $1,999 cash a new white 1966 Ford Mustang.

Two of my students, Gregory Thompson and Savannah Ann Cooper, were about to take me into worlds that I had never known. Savannah would lead me, hand in hand, into her world of abuse. Gregory Thompson was about to try to take our lives.

Chapter Nine

On the first day working for Burnside-Ott, I was excited about the planes as well as the opportunity to be a certified flight instructor. It was a great feeling to be able to help students learn the art of flying using their stick and rudder skills.

There was another feeling of excitement which came in the form of a woman, Savannah Ann Cooper.

Savannah was my first love in elementary school. She would ride on the handlebars of my bike around the small town of Coconut Grove. The year was 1946.

Burnside-Ott opened their doors in the mid-60s. It had been a long time since Savannah and I last saw each other. Even stranger than our chance meeting was the secret world that she had experienced. Hers was an internal torture, a psychological struggle all these years. It was a struggle that many could not understand unless they, too, had been in a similar place. It was a sequence of ups and downs when she was blamed when things went wrong, causing feelings of shame, guilt, and worthlessness in the depths of her soul.

Savannah's world was one of abuse. Her abuse began with her parents, but it did not end there.

"Come on Savannah! There will be pretty flowers and beautiful music! What is taking you so long!" Savannah Ann Cooper was five-years-old.

Savannah sat at her bedroom desk looking in the small mirror in front of her. Her bedroom window had laced curtains and opened blinds. Getting up from her desk, she walked away from the mirror and into the living room where her mother stood waiting with her arms folded.

"What did you do to your hair? Did you run a broom through it? Get back to your room! Don't come out until you do it right. Now hurry because we are running out of time!"

"Yes, Mama, I am sorry, I'll do it right this time."

"I hope so. Now, hurry up!"

Savannah was never sure what "Do it right" would mean. She was constantly trying to please everyone wondering what they wanted her to do. She would feel foolish each time she did things the way they should not have been done. Shame always flooded over her in those situations.

"Savannah! I told you to hurry up! We will be late and it will be your fault! Remember this! I have told you over and over! You are not allowed to close the bathroom door. You don't have anything that we have not seen! We all have a body. Another thing I want you to remember when I tell you.

Do not close your bedroom blinds. Can't you see when you don't listen how it leaves the house in a mess? Now hurry up!"

Savannah felt her face turn red with shame as she walked out of her room toward the front door with her mother.

"Mom is my hair okay?"

"No! But it will have to do!"

She followed her mother down the steps toward her father who had been waiting in the car.

The gray 1953 Dodge arrived at the Southside Methodist Church. Walking though the huge wooden double doors, they were met by the scent of fresh flowers. Flowers were everywhere. Colors of yellow, orange, and red mixed together into the green leaves of the arrangements. Groups of flower arrangements were placed around a small table in front of the altar.

On top of the altar was a photograph in a bright silver metal frame. Savannah and her parents sat near the front row to better hear everything.

Her father touched her leg so that he could make sure that he had her attention. She recoiled at his touch, but Savannah never understood why as she sat quietly beside him. "Remember Savannah you are not to talk and embarrass us."

She whispered back, "Okay Daddy."

Behind the bright silver-framed table with the photograph on top, a tall thin man stood in a dark suit. As he began speaking, Savannah sat up straight to show she was paying attention.

"We are gathered here today to honor the life of Johnathan Westly Theed. Johnathan, a young hero whose life was ended too soon, was loved and will be missed by all of us. His life was taken in the performance of his duty as an Air Force fighter pilot. His Mustang P-51 fighter plane was destroyed by enemy fire just after take off. Johnathan and his plane went down in a ball of fire hitting the ground only one mile from the end of the runway. His life was ended in protection of us all. We will all miss him dearly."

A tear flowed down Savannah's face as she sat still in silence. She felt guilty of having killed young Johnathan Theed when she heard the Preacher say, "His life was ended in protection of us all."

The colors of the flowers seemed to turn into black and white. The Preacher's words turned into slow motion as he continued.

"I know we will all miss Johnathan. My sympathy goes out to his family and friends that are gathered here today. Now, I would like to give you the opportunity to say something about our beloved hero Johnathan Westly Theed."

Savannah felt her eyes get puffy once again. Each person who came up spoke of how much he would be missed and how much he was loved by them. Finally, the last person to speak was Savannah's father. Standing behind the silver framed table and uniformed photo of Johnathan, he pointed to the photograph.

"This man was the finest person I have ever known. I never had to tell him to do the same thing twice. He always thought of others first and seemed to know of your needs before being asked. There is no one in this world who can take his place. My love for him, and the love of my family for him, will never leave our hearts or be replaced by the love of another."

Sitting there in silence next to her mother, she felt the deep inward pain of always needing that love that her father spoke of. It was a love that she too would constantly keep trying to prove to her family. A love that she never felt worthy of. She started sniffling, wiping her nose with the back of her tiny hand. She felt that it was her responsibility to have saved Johnathan, just as it was always her responsibility to take care of her family.

Her mother leaned over and whispered in her ear, "Savannah! What is wrong with you! Don't be such a baby. Don't wipe your nose with your hand. Where are your manners?"

"Sorry Mom, I will try to do better."

The church filled with organ cords and lyrics of *America The Beautiful*, as people sang "with purple mountains majesty and amber waves of grain" to honor their hero. It was beautiful. Savannah's trembling chin and the tears flowing down her young face found her mother digging through her purse for tissues.

"You are such a mess," her mother whispered reaching into her purse. Her mother touched a small fabric doll, took it out of her purse, and handed it to Savannah. "Here! Take this doll! Your cousin Johnathan, the war hero, left it at our house when he was about your age. I was going to give it to his mother. You can have it, just stop that foolish crying."

Savannah clutched the small fabric doll. It had been made into the shape of a parachute man from military khaki uniform cloth. A small parachute was stuffed into a pocket sewn on the back of his uniform. A darker brown cap was sewn over his head. Khaki goggles, the color of his uniform, had two blue eyes looking through them. The doll was worn from years of play by her cousin and its stuffing was visible through a tiny seam on its right arm.

"Now stop that foolish sobbing and dry your face. That little doll thing will always keep you safe. No need to cry. He has a parachute on his back that you can use to never get hurt. It keeps him from falling to the ground."

Savannah held the little parachute man tightly in her hands. "I will call you Johnathan Westly Theed" she whispered in its ear.

After the service, they walked back to the 1953 gray Dodge. Savannah's father opened the door for her mother, while Savannah climbed into the backseat. Once they were in, her father sat in the driver's seat looking back at her in the rearview mirror.

"Savannah?"

"Yes Dad?"

"I noticed you were crying."

"Yes Dad."

"You were in a church."

"Yes Dad."

"If you had any faith, you would not be crying in a church."

"Yes, Dad. I am sorry."

Savannah felt the pain of what had happened to her cousin and how he was loved and would be missed by all of those who spoke about him. Now, she knew even God was angry with her for not having enough faith.

They drove away in the gray Dodge, sitting in silence on the plain gray cloth seats and interior. As the car traveled down the black asphalt streets of town, Savannah sat watching the telephone wires between the poles. The wires seemed to sink away from the poles, rise to meet the next pole, and sink away again. She felt like she was rising and falling like the wires as she held tightly on to Johnathan Westly Theed.

They drove into the driveway, walked up to the front door, opened the door, and walked into the living room.

Sitting down on the couch, her father prepared a movie projector that was left out on the coffee table. Mother pulled the curtains closed and turned off the light attached to the ceiling fan. The bright shaft of light from the projector illuminated a place on the living room wall. The light on the wall was transformed into a flash of her cousin's bright silver aluminum P-51 Mustang.

He stood by the plane, waved, and climbed into the cockpit. Puffs of smoke came from the exhaust as the huge propeller began to rotate. Seconds later, he raced down the runway, black tires inches above the ground. Suddenly, the tires and landing gear were sucked up, disappearing into the bottom of the plane.

This time there would be no fireball explosion sending the plane and her cousin into the ground. She visualized her cousin in his uniform who had made the family so proud. She saw him covered in fire and screaming in pain. That pain that pierced her own young five-year-old heart and soul. She started to cry.

"Go to your room! Stay there until you are told to come out! We told you to stop that crying!" her mother demanded.

In the darkness of her bedroom that night, she felt the clean white sheets around her body. Mother had come in checking to make sure she had arranged her shirts, pants, and socks in the proper drawers and in the proper order. Mother always wanted to make sure that her daughter had done a good job. When she left the room, Savannah was pleased that her mother didn't say anything indicating that she had failed. She was pleased that she had satisfied her mother.

Looking through the open blinds of her bedroom window as she lay in bed, she saw a star piercing through the pitch blackness of night. Next to her chest, she clutched her little parachute man. A single tear flowed down her cheek falling on her little doll. She knew that, believing what her mother had said, her doll would keep her safe as she struggled with the constant ridicule and her failure to please her parents. She would try to do better.

Chapter Ten

Savannah's childhood appeared to be behind her.

She was working behind the scheduling desk matching students and instructors with their assigned airplanes. Her magnetic personality kept the students, as well a staff, enthralled with her charm and the beauty of her face and body. They had no idea that she was on a mission to please God. It was a mission to not make Him angry. She was not searching for any romantic encounters. In fact, her fourth marriage had been working well and appeared to be successful. She always seemed to look right through a person and deep into their soul. Her soft shoulder length light-red hair framed her face. Her enthusiastic smile accentuated her charm even more than usual on that day.

This wasn't the first time that I met Savannah Ann Cooper. The first time was at Coconut Grove Elementary School in First Grade.

We had a Christmas tree in our classroom. Mrs. Clark, our teacher, made little ornaments with the name of each child in her room attached to each ornament. We then picked a name from the tree and purchased a gift for that classmate.

Savannah chose my name. Her mother purchased a gender-neutral gift. While all my classmates had guns and trucks for the boys and dolls for the girls, I sat in my seat looking at the package that Savannah was holding out for me to take.

There she stood next to my desk with her red hair and freckles dotting her face. She looked as if she never had any food to eat and was as thin as a tooth pick even for a first-grade kid. She handed me something that I had no idea how to use. The gift was not a truck or gun like the other boys had. It was a game of Jax. Even worse she made it clear that she liked me. Yuck.

Pan American World Airways took me away from Savannah Ann Cooper. Our family was transferred to California for my father to fly their Pacific route.

Returning to Florida years later, I rediscovered Savannah when she was walking along Grand Avenue in the middle of Coconut Grove. It would have been difficult to miss her.

This time she was not the thin, red-headed kid with freckles. She was stunning; beautiful enough that she had been chosen to work as a model to promote Miami Beach.

I fell deeply in love with her. We would ride my bike with her sitting on the handlebars. As I stood on the walkway to the front of her home, we had our very first kiss.

Pan American once again took me away from Savannah. This time my family was transferred to Long Island, New York. My father would be flying the European routes.

Rumor had it that Savannah had married an older guy who was old enough to own a car. He married her, but after a year he committed suicide. After that, she was married three more times. There was always something in her relationships that made her feel insecure.

She had done everything in her power to keep her parents happy and her three marriages successful. It never seemed to be enough. Even God must be angry with her inability to do anything right.

Fear of rejection and failure learned at an early age kept her off balance. It was impossible for her to reflect on her experience or to feel anything. That lack of being able to feel was exacerbated by not being able to handle the conflict that had become her every day life. She was constantly trying to understand her failure with others and the fool she felt she had become. When she heard, "We are all sinners" she knew that even God must be angry with her for failing. She found herself reading her Bible more to find out what God wanted her to do for Him. She would awake at five in the morning every day to read her devotionals so that she would not make God become like her family—a God that was always unsatisfied and angry with her.

Savanna Ann Cooper—the Miami Beach model, the first girl that I had ever loved, and my first kiss—stood behind the scheduling desk at Burnside-Ott, trying to organize flight instructors with our students.

"Hi there," she said, flirting with me to have fun knowing that friends from the first grade, especially boyfriends, were difficult to find.

"Hi Savannah," came my reply, pretending not to look too interested as I walked past her.

"Rob, one day I would like to see what this flying thing is all about," she shouted through the crowd of students and instructors around the scheduling desk.

"Have you ever flown before?" I shouted back.

"No, never have."

"Well, we'll have to fix that."

"My cousin flew during the war," she volunteered as evidence that she knew something about flying.

"What kind of airplane did your cousin fly?"

"A P-51 Mustang. I was just a little kid then."

"Amazing, Savannah, my original Flight Instructor was also a P-51 Mustang fighter pilot. Oh, by the way, I was also just a little kid then."

"Gee, Rob, we have so much in common," she flirted with a playful smile. We once did, I thought, watching her as she took time to think about flying.

"Rob, I wouldn't know what to do or where to begin," she said, glancing around the room as if looking for answers from the experienced flight instructors.

"Savannah, if you would like, we could go up, do a few gentle turns, and make it a short flight."

"That is what I am afraid of."

"Gentle turns?"

"No, isn't a short flight the same as a crash?"

"Very funny, but actually you have a point. It might be well for you to realize that you will be flying with a certified professional flight instructor—a professional flight instructor who will not allow you to crash."

"Okay, Professional Flight Instructor, when and where?"

"In fact, I own a plane. It's a Citabria—airbatic spelled backwards—and we can go up to see if you like it."

"Oh no! No aerobatics!"

"Okay, no aerobatics. We'll do some gentle turns and straight and level flight for the first hour. Did you forget already that I am a professional flight instructor?"

"How could I forget? You keep reminding me." Savannah's smile once more lit up the room. Turning away, I walked toward the door and the flight line.

"Where and when?" she shouted.

"Well, today is your lucky day. Richards Field, 9 a.m. tomorrow on our day off," I said smiling.

"Nine a.m. tomorrow, Richards Field, I know where that is. Should I learn anything about stall speed and stalls that I keep hearing about? What is the stall speed of your Citabria?"

"Don't know, never looked, see you tomorrow at 9 a.m."

Chapter Eleven

The gentle onshore breeze from the southeast and Biscayne Bay swept across the farm land kissing the wet blades of grass at Richards Field at 9 a.m. the next morning.

We climbed into the airplane, fastened our seatbelts, and soon we were flying over the countryside of Homestead, Florida.

Savannah held the flight controls with a light touch starting to become at ease with her new surroundings. Warm air rising from the hot Florida land, known as a thermal, lifted the right wing.

"What did I do wrong?" she screamed letting go of the controls and grabbing the seat cushion under her with both hands.

"That was just a thermal lifting the right wing. Since you let go, and I am not flying the plane, it appears to be flying all by itself. You didn't do anything wrong. In fact, you could probably make the plane feel happier if you gave it your attention by holding on to the controls."

"Very funny, Rob. Now what do you want me to do?"

She gently placed her hands and feet back on the controls. It was more to please me than to fly the plane. After the thermal, it became impossible for her to relax.

"Savannah, I'll give you a chance to relax. I'll take the controls and fly back to Richards Field."

"Okay."

"How do you like flying an airplane?"

"It's fun," she laughed as if her laughter would convince me that she enjoyed flying. She gave a thumbs-up to convince me she was enjoying herself.

During the landing and then after the flight, and after we rolled the Citabria into the hangar, there was not much conversation. I guess Savannah expected me to ask her something about our flight that she felt she could not answer.

The next morning the darkness was illuminated by orange lasers of sunlight spiking through the towering cumulus clouds to the east.

Savannah was standing behind the scheduling desk when I arrived. She picked up her new Pilot Log Book and handed it to me. "You didn't sign this."

"Thanks, I'll fill in your first flight lesson. Savannah, it looks like we can scratch my first student off today's schedule. He's already twenty minutes late."

"Rob, you are open after him if he shows up late."

As soon as she finished talking, student pilot Gregory Thompson—six-foot- tall with a football player frame, came through the door. He appeared to have been a body builder. This was my first time flying with him, but he had soloed with another instructor, so at least I knew he could fly.

"Greg, I was about to give up on you."

"Yeah, I know, I was out partying last night," he said with a slight slur.

"Greg, you realize that drinking and flying don't mix?"

"Yeah, I know. We stopped drinking early last evening."

"I'll join you soon. Go out and preflight November 9098 Xray. It's the red and white Cessna 150 on the second row of planes."

Without a word, Greg turned and, once again, blocked the light coming through the school's doorway. He appeared slow to respond to his own body movements. Probably the booze from last night, I thought.

Realizing I was angry at him for his late arrival, I tried not to be judgmental or irritable about his lack of responsibility.

"November 9098 Xray cleared for take off."

"98 Xray, cleared for takeoff" Greg replied.

We were off into the wild blue yonder to see what Greg could do or how he could handle an airplane after a night of drinking.

We leveled off at 2,500 feet. The farm fields just west of New Tamiami Airport passed below.

"Greg, let's do some slow flight maintaining 2,500 feet."

Without a word, Greg lowered the flaps all the way down to 40 degrees. Instead of decreasing the airspeed, he was lowering the nose of the plane and the airspeed was increasing.

"Greg, your airspeed is increasing. Raise the nose slightly and watch your airspeed to maintain slow flight."

Greg over-controlled by raising the nose up too much causing the plane to drop out from under us in a stall.

"Greg, since we have already done a stall, let's try another one with full power." It was my plan to make the best of a bad situation.

Without a word, he raised the flaps, added full power, and began pulling back on the control yoke. The plane stalled. Greg pushed the control yoke full forward. We were pushed up out of our seats hard against the seat belts. Greg didn't realize what he had done, but continued to push the control yoke full forward.

The vertical dive brought the green and brown fields below racing toward the Cessna's windshield. My body froze and then grabbed for the controls. With a clenched jaw from the vexation caused by Greg's unresolved problems, I was about to give up on him.

Mounting frustration, and a touch of anger flowed over my body for allowing myself to fly with Greg after he had admitted to a night of drinking. It was obvious that it was affecting his flying. He had been signed off for solo so I knew he could do the simple maneuvers that I had requested of him. Those simple maneuvers that he had failed so badly.

The problem now had become my state of mind as well as Greg's poor performance. How could I get him to respond more appropriately on the controls?

"Greg, have you ever done a spin?"

"Yes, I like them," came his response as his voice sounded slow and deliberate.

"Great! Give me a one turn spin to the left."

Once more in silence, he pulled out the carburetor heat control, closed the throttle, applied full back pressure on the yoke, and full left rudder at the stall. The plane immediately dropped off into a spin with the earth rotating below.

Three quarters of the way around the turn Greg applied full opposite rudder. The spinning farm fields below suddenly froze in place as he released back pressure on the yoke and the plane returned to level flight.

His control of the plane was smooth and deliberate. The Cessna 150 had performed an aerial ballet. The plane recovered precisely at the point of entry. The maneuver was perfect. My judgment of Greg was misguided. He had performed perfectly. There was a feeling of euphoria about his success and my own accomplishment to have made that happen.

"Greg! Perfect! Good job!"

He showed no emotion, turning his glance slowly toward me. His vision locked on to my side of the cockpit as if he was looking out of the window.

"AHAA!" his scream filled the cockpit. Turning away from him to try to find the problem, my heart raced. I expected an imminent mid-air collision. My hands became clammy from fear. I turned quickly to look out my side.

Clear blue. The sky was an empty clear blue. All the way to the horizon there was not another plane in sight! The sky was empty. Turning back to Greg's huge frame filling the tiny Cessna 150 cockpit, what I saw was terrifying.

His eyes had rolled back into his head with only the whites showing. A white froth foamed out of his mouth. The white sticky substance was stringing out onto the yoke in front of him and beginning to cover the instrument panel. He began to rock forward pushing the control yoke with him. Suddenly, the plane went into a 500-foot dive. Then, he rocked back pulling the yoke with him forcing the plane into a 500-foot climb. Grabbing the controls, I found them locked in my student's strong grip. Even the throttle was locked in his grip at half throttle. What was I to do? The airplane controls were locked in my student's hands while he went through a kind of seizure.

In a state of shock, I remembered Charlie Burr's yellow J-3 Cub where fresh air would come through the open fold down door. After the passing storm, I remembered his words of instruction, "Go ahead and fly it."

"What do I need to do?"

"Just give it what it needs."

Then, another stronger voice seemed to shout at me. That voice was the old P-51 fighter pilot, "What the hell are you waiting for? Fly the damn plane. I don't want to be picking up body parts and airplane pieces."

My body felt heavy and numb. My brain was scrambling to find a logical solution to an illogical situation. Slowly a vision came to me of old World War I biplanes with their engines at full throttle which were shut down completely to enable their pilots to control altitude. With Greg's hand locked around the throttle, I could pull the mixture control and starve the engine of fuel to lose altitude and put the plane in a glide.

Reaching for the red knob of the mixture control, I pulled it out. The engine went quiet. Pushing the knob back in, the engine came back to life. The altitude could be controlled by turning the engine on and off. The only exception would be the 500-foot of altitude gain and loss as Greg continued rocking back and forth pushing and pulling the control yoke with him.

Feeling I had semi-control of the plane, I grabbed the control yoke and placed my feet on the rudder pedals, but they were locked solid by Gregg's body.

As I watched Greg rock and move the yoke with him, I noticed that his fingers left a small amount of play as they were forced against each other. The yoke could be turned, only slightly, between his locked fingers.

The construction of the New Tamiami Airport was visible in the distance. I saw the yellow earth-moving equipment in the distance as small specks near the horizon. Clouds of dust billowed up around the plows as they moved the earth. If we crashed near the machines, I knew someone would see us go down and come rescue us.

Savannah stood behind the scheduling desk. The radio frequency behind her was always turned on to monitor planes and instructors should they be running late.

"Burnside-Ott this is November 9098 Xray, can anyone hear me?"

"November 98 Xray. Is that you Rob?" Savannah's voice answered back.

"Affirmative, 98Xray is having some difficult."

"98Xray are you going to be late for your next student?"

"I am afraid so. My student is locked on the controls!"

"What?"

"He is unconscious and locked onto the controls!"

"Are you declaring an emergency?"

"Negative. It would not do any good."

"What are you going to do?"

"Hope to see you later Savannah."

She stood in shock and disbelief of how this could be happening.

"November 9098Xray, this is Savannah. Rob, can you hear me?"

The silence found her standing all alone. She remembered her first-grade love. The time she felt embarrassed of his disappointment looking at the gift of a package of Jax. Then there was the time riding on the handle bars of his bike. She remembered the fun they had and how somehow he seemed to be the only person who never demanded her to do better. He never knew how deeply she had been in love with him even after the First Grade. She remembered how she had finally found a happy marriage after three failed ones. Her fourth husband Dave made her feel special. He never made demands of her and that counted so much.

"November 9098 X-ray, do you hear me? This is Savannah."

The silence filled the room. Her heart pounded with the thought of what might be happening to her friend Rob. A single tear was quickly wiped away before it could roll down her cheek. She felt confused. Why had she not waited for him instead of getting married at such a young age to her first husband? That husband had become so abusive. None of that mattered now. Time had placed different people in their lives, different people that they were now married to.

Savannah silently prayed that Rob would return safely. If he didn't, a part of her would die with him. That part of her that was still in the First Grade. That part of her before she was always trying to be accepted by her family and abusive husband. That unconditional love she had found riding on the handlebars and her first kiss. She felt confused. She had found unconditional love with Dave, but still her first-grade experience with love could not be forgotten.

"98Xray can you hear me? Rob, this is Savannah. Can you hear me?" Once again, silence filled the room.

Making a slight turn toward the New Tamiami Airport with the slight amount of movement available in the locked control yoke, I pulled the fuel mixture and the engine went silent.

A mental numbness found me reaching for the door handle of the Cessna in desperation. Starting to unfasten my seat belt, there was a self-loathing and anger loaded with disgust at what I was about to do.

Glancing at the altimeter, I saw that it read 1,500 feet. It would be a quick death, but what about my student? Removing my hand from the door handle, I tightened my seatbelt, feeling the slime as it spread to my side of the cockpit.

Somehow, there was resolve at not opening the door and plunging to my death. There was hope. There was control of altitude, plus or minus 500 feet, by using the mixture control for power. There was also a slight amount of control using the yoke. By using the limited control of the yoke, we were headed toward the unfinished New Tamiami Airport.

Keeping the plane lined up with the distant airport through skidding turns and the loss and gain of altitude, we were finally overhead looking down at the yellow land clearing machines. A small amount of left yoke and we started a skidding turn over the airport turning the plane enough to line up with runway 9 Left. Our altitude was 1,000 feet. With a pounding heart and noticing once more my sweaty hands, I waited on the 500-foot roller coaster dive that would take us closer to the runway and the portending crash.

As I pulled the red knob of the fuel mixture, the engine became silent. The sound of the outside air could be heard as the dive toward the ground began. A tingling in my arms, tightened chest, and accelerated breathing swept over my body as I awaited the crash. Wing flaps were lowered all the way to slow the impact. The black newly applied asphalt of the runway rushed toward the windshield. Instinctively, I turned my body sideways away from the impending crash that would push us into the instrument panel, killing us both.

Greg slowly began to rock back pulling the yoke with him. The view of the runway began to look like a normal approach to landing. Getting to within inches above the new asphalt, Greg decreased the rocking as the tires began sliding on the surface of the new runway.

Remembering back to my early days of flight instructing, I had witnessed a fatal airplane crash. We watched as the pilot's airplane had a complete power failure. He tried to turn back toward the airport, but did not have enough altitude. The plane disappeared below the trees and we hurried to try to help him. The plane had struck the trees pushing the engine back into his lap, killing him. His eyeballs had been pushed out and were hanging on his cheeks.

In another second, we could be doomed to have our body parts and aircraft pieces scattered across the runway. We were on the ground, but the landing was not over. The plane was sliding out of control toward the runway lights on the right side of the runway. Greg's toes were locked on the toe brakes. The new asphalt helped us slide to a stop inches from the edge of the runway. We had landed. We were safe!

Grabbing the Cessna's door handle, I threw open the door as if I was escaping from a jail cell. A cloud of dust seemed to come from nowhere, suddenly surrounding me and the Cessna. The yellow ground clearing machine operator sat above looking down toward me.

"We have a problem!" I screamed.

"I'll take you to the Foreman's shack so you can make a phone call. Climb up," the operator shouted. Climbing onto the side of the yellow machine, I hung on for dear life as the wind circled my body. I was feeling good to be alive.

The first call was to get an ambulance for my student. The second call was to Burnside-Ott for them to relay the message to Savannah that things had worked out and that I was okay. Don Burnside wanted to know if the plane could be flown back to the airport. I assured him that it could. There was nothing wrong with the plane now that Gregg was not hampering the controls.

The unfinished asphalt was solid enough for take off. Adding full power, the Cessna raced by the operator sitting by the side of the runway on his machine. He waved as I lifted into the sky. With a turn to the northeast, I leveled off at 1,000 feet.

Greg had suffered a grand mal epileptic seizure. He remained unconscious that day, through the night, and half of the next day. Although he had a current medical certificate, he would never fly again.

With the landing completed, the routine instructions from the tower indicated that it should have been just another normal hour of dual flight instruction, "98Xray cleared to the ramp."

Adding a slight amount of power, I turned down the parallel taxiway leading to Burnside-Ott's tie down area. Once there, I pulled the mixture to idle cut off. The propeller slowed to its final compression stroke freezing in a straight up position. The ramp seemed unusually quiet. There were no planes moving, flight instructors doing pre-flights, or even line support staff. Securing 98Xray and slowly walking toward the flight school office once again, I felt relieved and enjoyed once again the feeling of being alive.

When I opened the door to the flight school office, I saw a long homemade paper sign made of taped together scheduling paper. Words printed on the sign said, "Welcome home Rob!"

Inside the office, the entire staff of Burnside-Ott Aviation Training Center formed two lines for me to walk through. "Welcome home Rob!" came their one loud shout while walking down the center of the two lines shaking hands and receiving pats on the back.

Arriving at the end of the lines, I came to Savannah Ann Cooper looking as perfect as usual. Her smile brightened the room. She held something out toward me in her hand. It was a small paper object. The paper was cut into the shape of one of those First-Place Blue Ribbons you would win at the local county fair.

Printed on the inside top of the round part of the "ribbon" was a small stick red airplane and above the stick airplane were the words, "HERO MEDAL."

On the bottom of the circle surrounding the stick airplane, I saw "FIRST PILOT TO LAND AT NEW TAMIAMI"

Savannah pinned the "Hero Medal" on my white dress shirt and hugged me. Not able to hold back any longer, she began to cry.

Over time, there were other awards. Flight Standards District Office (FSDO) Miami, Florida, "Flight Instructor of The Year" and the "Wright Brothers Master Pilot Award" for "Demonstrating professionalism, skill, and aviation expertise, by maintaining safe operations for 50 or more years."

Through the years, it became obvious to me that it was not about my own achievements, but also the achievements of my students. My students would go on to become Air Force jet fighter Pilot Instructors, Crop Dusters, Banner Towers, and, yes, even the sought-after position of Airline Pilot. Many followed me as Certified Flight Instructors, sharing their knowledge and skills with others.

Indeed, it became obvious that not only was it not about my achievements, it was about the truth that was found even while flying with Greg, my epileptic student. There was no stronger illustration to prove:

"My grace is sufficient for you, for my strength is made perfect in weakness, therefore most gladly I will boast in my weakness, that the power of Christ may rest upon me" 2 Corinthians 12:9 (MEV). There was no other answer, at least in my mind, for me to be alive. Once in a small sailboat as a foolish teenager, then in an out of control airplane with locked flight controls, God had been, and was in control, during my own weakest moments.

There is a quote from an unknown author. It pertains to my brush with death while flying in an airplane with locked controls. It is also applicable to Savannah Ann Cooper and her own internal struggle with demons from her abuse.

"When God pushes you to the edge, trust Him fully because only two things can happen: Either He will catch you when you fall or He will teach you to fly."

FIRST PILOT TO LAND AT "NEW" TAMIAMI

HERO MEDAL

May 6, 1966

TO WHOM IT MAY CONCERN

On May 5, 1966 _____ developed a seizure and frothing after reviewing private pilot airwork(with exception of 720 power turns for approved school) and executing a one turn spin (360° duration) recovering successfully to straight and level flight.

After he became rigid on the controls and began frothing, the Flight Instructor, R.G. Mixon, recovered the controls and executed and emergency forced landing at the "New" Tamiami Airport, which was completed "dead stick" approach, full flaps, and brakes locked due to precautions of a landing with full power, with student jammed against controls, and flaps to decrease impact speed if situation became worse. It was not known that the brakes were fully locked until touch down which was smooth enough to prevent wheels digging in.

The student was then taken to Baptist Hospital, (after a report was given to Metro Police) for observation and the aircraft was flown back to Tamiami. The carburator heat was found inoperative prior to the forced landing due to a broken cable occuring that hour of flight.

R.G. Mixon
CFI 1585409

Homemade "Hero Medal" made at the flight school after an emergency landing at New Tamiami Airport which was under construction after a student had an epileptic seizure while flying.

98

Chapter Twelve

The early morning aroma of coffee filled the office. Savannah stood behind the scheduling counter as usual. She glanced up as I walked in. "Good morning Rob," she greeted me, adding her usual smile.

"Good morning, Savannah. I know we are scheduled to fly today in the school's Cessna, but before we go up let's talk about it."

"You sound very professional."

"Yes, I have my Instructor's hat on."

We entered the small conference room behind the scheduling counter. The door was closed for privacy.

"Savannah, you seemed more than slightly uncomfortable when we last flew."

"Did I do something wrong?" she asked with her eyes suddenly looking at the floor in embarrassment.

"No, not at all. Learning is a process. Having said that, I have to ask you if you really want to learn to fly an airplane."

She looked up for a moment and then looked back down toward the floor. "Are you angry with me?" Her usual smile faded into a blank stare.

"When we flew in the Citabria, you seemed more concerned about pleasing me than learning to fly the plane. It's not about me."

It's always about others, she thought. The kids next door when I was left home alone. How they chased me with a small battery and cables to shock me. Throwing me to the floor, rubbing against me when I was helpless on the floor and they were on top of me. I couldn't tell my parents because they would say it was my fault. They always talked highly of the boys next door.

"I knew it! I made you mad. You are disappointed with me." I can never do anything right."

"Savannah, no I am not mad or disappointed. It is not about me, but it is about you learning to fly the plane."

She looked up as if in self-defense, "Not disappointing people is a good thing. What is wrong with not wanting to disappoint others? Others should be more important than yourself."

She sat in silence remembering her son sitting in a reclining chair in front of the television. How she brought him a tray of food prepared especially for him. How he didn't touch or taste the food but said, "This food is too hot." How she felt obligated to run back to the kitchen to cool off the food. She had even made her husband and two sons so angry that they punched holes through the wall inches from her head. How could she not care about others? It was always about others. It was always about how she was never good enough or smart enough. Once again, she felt so foolish for not getting things right. Shame flooded over her entire body as she looked down at the floor.

"I don't understand" she said pressing her hands to her temples. "You don't want to fly with me?"

"Of course, I want to fly with you. Flying an airplane can teach you lots of things about yourself, in addition to just learning to fly. Before we fly, I need to know if you really want to learn to fly an airplane."

"Okay, yes, let's go flying." she said with her customary smile returning once again.

"By the way Savannah, what did you say was the reason that you wanted to learn to fly?"

She made direct eye contact remembering her little parachute man that she always carried in her purse.

"I didn't say," came her matter of fact answer. Getting up from the conference table we walked out of the room into the scheduling area.

A flight instructor was listening to one of his students who asked, "What is the stall speed of the Cessna 150?"

Before the instructor could answer, Savannah smiled pointing back to me, "I know of an instructor who would tell you, 'Don't know, never looked'" she laughed. "I am sure your instructor will have a more definitive answer than that!"

We walked through the door out toward the flight line. November 5096 Xray was a blue and white new Cessna 150. The paint and interior looked as though it had never been touched. It had that new plane smell that flooded outside once the door was opened.

"I don't remember anything from when we flew your plane."

"Just start the preflight routine inside of the cockpit to make sure all of the electrical switches are turned off after you lower the flaps."

"Your airplane didn't have flaps."

"No, it didn't"

"Where are the flap switches?"

Her face turned red with embarrassment. She felt like a fool again. Once again, she felt the humiliation that whatever the situation, she would be criticized for doing something wrong.

She lowered her eyes to look down at the black asphalt. All she ever wanted to do was please others and she never even seemed to get that right. She looked up toward me with a single tear running down her face.

"Savannah, you didn't do anything wrong. You don't have to do this. We don't have to fly today."

I don't want you to be angry with me for being so stupid. I can't remember what it is that you want me to do."

"That's okay," I assured her. "I can't remember what we are supposed to do either. Let's get in the plane. We can discover how not to be perfect."

She didn't want anyone to know. It wasn't just about flying an airplane. It was about exchanging the void of not having feelings. Those feelings that she had never been allowed to have, feelings others considered foolish. She never seemed to please others no matter how hard she tried. Her shame was trapped inside of having her clothes ripped off by her husband in front of her children as they watched. The shame of having a plate broken over her head for preparing the wrong food. Her mother's voice saying, "At least he didn't hit you this time."

For a second, she visualized her hero cousin climbing into his P-51. Her plane was only a Cessna 150, but it was an airplane with a cockpit just the same. Perhaps, she, too, could earn the love and respect she had seen and heard at her cousin's funeral.

Inside the cockpit, she buckled her seatbelt. Taking the "Before Starting Check List" that was handed to her, she began checking the items off. When she finished the list, the engine roared to life.

Once over the practice area of isolated farm fields, we were flying level at 2,000 feet.

"Okay, now that we have the plane trimmed and level, let's let go of all of the controls and see what happens."

"Both of us?"

"Both of us," came my reply. I held both hands up above my head to let her see that the plane could fly by itself.

"Savannah, see how the plane will fly by itself? Gently, hold onto the controls and keep both wing tips level on the outside horizon just like they are now. A slight amount of stick and rudder will turn the plane if you want to try a turn."

"That is okay. I think I will just fly straight and level for now."

Looking at the left wingtip, she moved the yoke to the left. The left wing dropped below the horizon.

"Take the plane! Rob take the plane. What did I do wrong?"

"You just moved the yoke in the direction that you were looking. Are you sure you want to do this?"

"Are you angry with me?"

"No, just relax and let the plane return to level flight. Now, let's try a shallow turn to the left. Just use a slight amount of left rudder and yoke to make the turn. Keep the nose of the plane where you have it on the horizon."

The plane slowly began a shallow left turn.

"Awesome. You did it. A perfect turn."

"Are you making fun of me?"

"Not at all. Now, try one to the right."

"How steep should I turn?"

"As steep as you feel comfortable."

"Will the plane turn over?"

"Not unless you want it to do that. It takes a lot of effort and skill to learn how to make a plane turn over."

As we sat in silence, once more Savannah felt insecure about being a failure. "Are you mad at me?"

"No, you are doing great. You are doing a good job with those turns. Why would you believe that I was mad at you?"

"It's the silence. When people are angry with me, they become silent. I guess I make them so angry that I am not worth talking to. I never thought of why, but it always makes me feel like I've done something wrong. At times, the silence went on for over a month in my house like I was not even there."

"No, I am not angry. Let's make a few more turns before we head back to the airport."

Savannah became more relaxed while sucking in a quick breath. With widened eyes of amazement, she looked over at me if only a glance. She wanted to see if I was experiencing the same excitement that she was feeling.

"I can't believe it." she screamed with joy. I am actually flying an airplane."

"Yes, Savannah, yes you are flying an airplane" came my reply through a smile at her accomplishment. She had not only flown an airplane, but she was lifted out of her world of negative expectations and into a new world of a positive reality.

Six hours had passed since her first flight lesson. Only one maneuver had brought her anxiety level up to near panic. That one maneuver was the power-on stall.

Our altitude was 3,000 feet. "Savannah, how do you feel about flying now?"

Just as before when she had mastered simple turns, she sucked in a deep breath, her eyes widened, and she looked at me sitting next to her.

"This is awesome! I never thought I would be able to fly a plane! Johnathan Westly Theed would be proud of me."

"Who is Johnathan Westly Theed?"

"Never mind Johnathan Theed."

"I don't know who this Johnathan Westly Theed is, but whoever he is I am sure he would be proud. Savannah, there is something I want you to think about."

"What is it?"

"It is a maneuver that is only required for Certified Flight Instructors. The maneuver is a one-turn spin. It is a maneuver that you will not want to do."

"How do you do it?" Will you show me one?"

"If I show you one, it might make you feel really scared. If you do one, it is easy. If I show you one, you have to promise to do the next one."

Without thinking Savannah said, "I promise!"

With power-off to start a glide, yoke pulled back into our lap, full left rudder and the earth below became a cyclone of green and brown. Opposite rudder, released back pressure on the yoke, and the earth below, in front of the plane, froze in place. Savannah held on to the seat cushion under her.

"Yeah! Right! You want me to do that!"

"Only if you want to, but remember you promised."

"Will you stay on the controls with me?"

"I will stay right behind you on the controls."

"Okay, here we go!"

Once again, this time as Savannah was talked through the maneuver, the earth became a blur of green and brown farm fields spinning below the plane. Then immediately, the plane froze the horizon in place exactly where the maneuver had begun.

"I did it! Did you help me?"

"No, you did it all by yourself."

"Can I do another one, Rob?"

"Sure, but this time I want you to explain how you are doing it when you do it."

"What?"

"Just pretend that I am your student."

"Sure, why not, I'll just tell you what I am doing when I do it."

"Exactly."

Once again, she completed the spin as she explained the maneuver. The exit was precisely on target at the point of entry. She had mastered an aerobatic maneuver to perfection. For the first time in her life, she felt in control. She had mastered a spin. She was flying an airplane.

"Savannah, are you okay?"

"Okay? I am great!"

"Let's try one more thing before we head back to the airport. Remember when you asked the stall speed of the Cessna 150 and I told you, "Don't know; never looked?"

"Yes I remember that."

"Okay, this time I want you to do a spin with an entry speed of 80 miles an hour. An airplane can stall at any airspeed. Give it a try."

Without a word, Savannah pulled hard all the way back on the control yoke at 80 mph. At the same time, she kicked the full left rudder, making the airplane snap to the left which put the plane upside down. The plane continued to roll from upside down to right side up with the right rudder stopping the movement in the completion of a snap roll.

"I see what you mean. An airplane can stall at any airspeed."

"Congratulations. You have just demonstrated a perfect Snap Roll."

"It was just like the spin, but instead of going down we just kept flying straight ahead."

"Exactly. By the way, the Cessna 150 is not approved for Snap Rolls so this will be just between you and me."

After we landed, Savannah reached into her brown cloth flight bag to find her pilot log book. Her fingers brushed against her little parachute man. "How proud he must be of me" she thought pulling her log book out of the bag and handing it to me to be signed.

"I am signing you off for precision spins. They are only required for becoming a Certified Flight Instructor."

"Certified Flight Instructor? You must be kidding." She laughed, "I am only a Student Pilot!"

"Correct! A Student Pilot with a Certified Flight Instructor spin endorsement! Let me run this by you Savannah to see what you think."

"What?"

"Since you enjoyed spins and mastered a Snap Roll, tomorrow I can bring my Citabria over from Richards Field to

Tamiami. You could learn some more aerobatics, but only if you are interested. Remember the Snap Roll in the Cessna 150 was only to show you that an airplane can stall at any airspeed. Only do approved maneuvers for the airplane you are flying."

"Interested. I am about to pee in my pants."

"Savannah! Southern ladies do not pee in their pants."

"They do if you excite them enough," she said, adding a wink and smile. She turned away from the plane and walked toward the office.

Before reaching the office, she felt a feeling flooding over her, but not a feeling of accomplishment. She remembered another time. A time when she felt as special as she had just felt mastering the aerobatic maneuvers. That time her first husband gave her a $200 dress. It was beautiful. He had needed her to wear the dress for "eye candy" to impress his friends. The dress was a long black dress that highlighted her curves. She soon discovered that it was not worn properly by her for him. In his sadistic manner, he showed his disapproval for not being sexy enough by following the incident with one and a half months of silence to prove to her how insignificant she had become. It was just one abusive treatment among the many that he had put her through.

Savannah's world had been a black and white world of only pleasing others. She was not allowed to have any feelings or needs of her own. She had been repeatedly scorned, first from her parents, then from her husband, and finally from her own children. Silence was a power that others could use against her.

Savannah Ann Cooper's life was about to change forever.

Chapter Thirteen

In the office, she opened her logbook and ran her fingers over every word of my endorsement for her spin accomplishment that I had written there. She proudly remembered how it happened: "I certify that Savannah Ann Cooper has received the required training of section 61.183 (I). I have determined that she is competent in instructional skills for training stall awareness, spin entry, spins, and spin recovery procedures. Robert G. Mixon, 1585409 CFI, ATP."

We climbed into the Citabria, adjusted our parachutes, buckled our seatbelts and shoulder harnesses. Picking up the Before Starting Checklist from inside of the door, she began reading it out loud: "Seat belts buckled, fuel on, mixture rich, master switch on, prime as required, magneto switches on, throttle cracked open, brakes set." Then putting her head near the open window, she yelled outside, "Clear prop!"

The engine roared to life. The wind from the propeller blasted through the open window. The cockpit filled with the smell of burned fuel from the exhaust. Savannah adjusted her David Clark headset into a more comfortable position, moving the microphone closer to her mouth. In the backseat of the Citabria, I moved my microphone closer to give her instructions.

"Savannah, at first you will feel like your arms are crossed when flying the Citabria. This is because the Cessna throttle was in your right hand and yoke in your left. It's the opposite in the Citabria. The Citabria control stick is in your right hand, throttle in your left on the left side of the cockpit."

"What?"

"Don't worry. It won't take long before the control stick feels more natural."

Savannah added power to taxi. The Citabria's small tail wheel slowly moved along the paved taxiway.

"Remember, just give it what it needs, no more, no less" came my instructions from the backseat over the cracking intercom.

She watched as the center line of the taxiway slowly moved directly under the center of the Citabria. A slight movement to the left suddenly turned into a swerve as she watched it happen.

"Oh shit! Rob, you've got the plane!" she exclaimed.

"No I don't. Just make small corrections as soon as they are needed. Just give it what it needs."

Savannah applied a slight amount of right rudder and the plane returned to the center line of the taxiway.

Lining up with the center line of the runway, she waited for the tower to clear her for takeoff.

"Citabria November 5909 Alpha cleared for takeoff."

"09 Alpha cleared for takeoff. We would like a straight-out departure."

"Understand 09 Alpha straight-out approved. Have a good flight."

She held onto the controls with a bit of apprehension knowing the possibility of a loss of directional control from her experience with taxiing. The Citabria, with a small steerable tail wheel, required much more attention to keep it straight than the Cessna 150 with its steerable nose wheel.

"Rob, I am as ready as I will ever be. Follow me through on the controls. I don't want to break your airplane."

"I am right behind you," came my reply from the backseat trying to ease Savannah's apprehension.

"Very funny."

The engine roared to life as she added full power. The runway center line began racing below the Citabria as we picked up speed. Slight forward pressure on the stick slowly lifted the small steerable tail wheel up off the surface of the runway. The rudder moved slightly to the right to keep the plane straight. Then it happened. With the rudder in neutral, the plane swerved to the left. Too much right rudder to compensate for the left turn made the plane swerve to the right.

"Oh shit! You've got the plane Rob."

"No, I don't. Just give it what it needs" I tried to assure her in a calm voice as the runway lights and edge of the pavement came racing toward the windshield.

She gently applied the necessary rudder to move the nose of the plane back toward the center of the runway. The plane's speed was increasing, tail in the air, and she applied a slight amount of back pressure on the stick to gently lift us into the sky. The runway lights on the side of the runway passed under the plane as it began to climb.

"Not too bad for your first try with a tail wheel airplane on a paved runway."

"That was terrible."

"We didn't crash, did we?"

"I am not sure I am still thinking about that. It almost made me pee in my pants." Her laughter filled the cockpit as she felt somewhat relieved that we had not actually crashed.

"Savannah, I have an idea."

"That's what I am afraid of. Okay Rob, what is your idea?"

"Go ahead and climb to 3,000 feet. We will get you ready for the Sebring, Florida aerobatic competition."

"We are going to fly to the Sebring contest?"

"Yes, and then you will fly in the contest!"

"Seriously? Are you crazy?"

"Seriously. Basic category only has three maneuvers and the one turn spin is the most difficult. You have already done the one turn spin."

"What are the other two maneuvers?"

"A Loop and a Roll."

"Sounds great, but what if I make a mistake?"

"Then you won't win. But with this plane, you won't win anyway. See, you have nothing to lose. They will allow a Safety Pilot to fly with you. That will be me. The Safety Pilot is not allowed to say anything or touch the controls."

Savannah smiled turning around to look at me in the backseat, "Well, a Safety Pilot who doesn't say anything or touch the controls will be nothing new."

Savannah felt a strange emptiness. All her life it had been up to her to make sure that everything worked for everyone else. Now, she was getting ready to fly in a contest that she could not win in an airplane that was outclassed by advanced aerobatic machines. In her emptiness, she felt a strange freedom. A freedom that allowed her to live without worrying about making mistakes. All of this in an environment that should have had strict boundaries of aerobatic performance the way her parents and husband had always imposed their demands on her.

The old Savannah all but disappeared. Her next words were more of a battle cry, "Rob! Let's do this!"

The plane was level at 3,000 feet. She listened carefully to my instructions, "Lower the nose to 140 miles an hour. Keep track of where the outside horizon is at all times so that you don't get lost in the maneuver."

The nose of the Citabria gently lowered for the entry into a loop. Airspeed increased to 140 miles an hour. Savannah applied smooth back pressure on the stick watching the nose climb above the horizon as we were pushed deep into our seats. The earth in front of us disappeared as clear, empty, blue sky appeared. Then, the earth reappeared up-side-down as we momentarily hung inverted from our seat belts. With the plane headed toward the ground, we were, once again, pushed deep into our seats watching the sky and earth return to their rightful positions.

Savannah's joy came over the headsets, "Wow! Awesome! We did it!"

"No Savannah, you did it!"

Her feelings of shame, guilt, and inadequacy were slowly slipping away in her new world of confidence with each successful aerobatic maneuver. She had no way of knowing my own feelings of inadequacy while flying with Lowry. Even before that, like her, my life was to try not to displease my father. She had no way of knowing that I, too, experienced severe punishment being beaten with the buckle of my father's belt for not picking up my toys. Mother's warning, "Wait 'till you father gets home!" found me feeling his anger when he returned home from a two-week trip. The black and blue marks faded after a few days. On the other hand, Savannah's marks were on the inside, etched deeply into her heart and soul. Even God had reasons to be angry with her, she often thought growing up.

She had no way of knowing that I, too. felt failure and embarrassment when I could never seem to please my father. He did not mean harm when he continued to remind me that, "The sign of a good mechanic is to not over-tighten something!" My failure of trying to get it perfect by turning the wrench one more turn, only to be disappointed by hearing the bolt "CRACK."

Then there was my own nakedness, like I was on display, when our family moved to another school before I could learn the Multiplication Tables. The new school had advanced into Division problems. My shame and ignorance filled the classroom when my new teacher had us compete in writing figures on the chalkboard in front of the entire class. Standing there with a piece of white chalk, I froze in shame as my team lost. While the other rows of students quickly wrote the answers to multiplication problems on the board, my own shame flooded over me.

"Okay, let's tie the three maneuvers together."

The plane sliced through the sky, engine roaring to 140 miles an hour, to near weightlessness at the top of the loop once again. Then we were pushed into our seats, as the plane smoothly pitched up above the horizon with an indicated airspeed of 120 miles an hour. Full left rudder and stick sent the horizon rolling inverted and then right-side-up. It was as if she had her hand on the horizon in front of the plane making it perform at her command. She was in control of her new world. Slowly, the airspeed decreased to just above stall. Then suddenly, as if a downward pulling tornado had the plane, the nose dropped away mastering the earth below into a perfect spin.

Sitting in silence, I watched as Savannah took control of her life piece by small piece. She would not have the fear of belt buckle beatings or Multiplication Tables. She would not have the embarrassment of an over-tightened bolt. Those things were nothing compared to her experiences. Her experience was far deeper than that.

She had been constantly ridiculed by her mother. She had had holes punched in the wall by her husband and son inches from her head, food that she cooked that was too hot, a dinner plate broken over her head because she prepared the wrong food, and the list went on until the only emotion she had left was the fear of constant failure and the fear of not being accepted.

Savannah Ann Cooper was about to compete against advanced aerobatic airplanes with experienced aerobatic competition pilots flying them. She was about to attack such admirable foes, and her own internal demons, all of this with only a Student Pilot's License.

Chapter Fourteen

Savannah climbed the yellow and white Citabria with its Star Burst paint design on the top of the wing and tail to 3,000 feet over the aerobatic Box in Sebring, Florida. She looked below to make sure that she was within the four corners marked with their white "L" shaped markers.

She lined up for her first maneuver. Lowering the nose of the plane, she rocked her wings with a "Wing-wag" indicating to the judges below that her aerobatic sequence was starting.

The engine roared as she picked up speed to 140 miles an hour. Then the loop was followed by 120 miles an hour for the next maneuver. After finishing the Slow Roll, she quickly checked the aerobatic box markers below. Flying outside of the box would determine a zero score.

In the backseat, I acted as her Safety Pilot, not saying a word, with a knowing grin as if bragging to myself of her accomplishments. Her increased confidence had her mentally fixating on the success of her previous maneuver while planning for the next. Her adrenaline was pumped up as if she were flying in a World Aerobatic Competition Championship.

She pushed forward on the control stick at the precise point to end her spin exactly at the point of entry with a perfect vertical downline. She returned to level flight rocking her wings with another "Wing-wag" indicating to the Line Judges that her aerobatic sequence was finished.

With the chirp of rubber meeting the pavement, Savannah landed the Citabria in front of the judges. She turned off the active runway and taxied down the taxiway to the tie down area. We unbuckled our seatbelts, shoulder harnesses, and parachutes. She turned around in the front seat to look at me as I sat there smiling at her.

"I was so nervous. I didn't want to make any mistakes!"

"Great job. No mistakes."

"I wonder how I did?"

"You don't have to wonder. Let's see if the judges have posted your score."

We walked behind the row of judges to the posting board. The results were printed on a long piece of white plain paper written in dark black ink. Pilot's names, type of aircraft, and then how they placed.

The first plane was a Pitts Special, second was an Extra 300, and then third was the name Savannah Ann Cooper flying a Citabria. Not only had she won Third Place, but she had also out flown two pilots who were flying superior aerobatic airplanes, a Pitts Special and an Extra.

Savannah Ann Cooper stood taller, walking with wide steps, as she walked past the more advanced flying machines and their pilots. There was an inner sense of calm. For the first time in her life, she knew there would still be struggles, but she felt at ease with her accomplishments.

"Once in a while someone amazing comes along and here I am!" using a direct quote from Tigger of *Whinny the Poo* fame, and adding her huge grin.

"Savannah, does that mean you feel good about your accomplishment?" I asked her.

"I feel awesome!" came her reply. Indicating that everything was as it should be in her new-found world.

That afternoon, orange rays of sunlight sent their bright colors up through the huge white cumulus clouds to the west. The clouds had started changing colors into a lighter orange as Savannah climbed into her car.

On the seat next to her, she had her cloth flight bag. Opening the bag, she placed her log book inside. Deep down in the darkness of the bag, she felt her little parachute man. It had been a long journey. Gently holding him with her finger tips, she brought him out from the dark and into the sunlight. She sat there in thought for some time holding her little parachute man close to her. The daylight faded into darkness as the western horizon flashed its last colors of orange into purple, then gray into night. She held her little parachute man up to her face. Her voice was a whisper as she told him, "Know that wisdom is such to your soul; If you find it, there will be a future and your hope will not be cut off" Proverbs 24:14 (ESV).

Little did I know that my own life was about to be filled with fear and uncertainty.

Pitts Special came in first during an aerobatic competition where Savannah Ann Cooper and I were competing in a Citabria. Savannah came in Third Place, but still won in her own world after dealing with abuse.

Chapter Fifteen

I glanced at the Citabria's altimeter. It showed 3,000 feet. The roar of the engine and g-force were like old friends. Weightlessness at the top of a loop and then the ground racing toward the windshield, like hundreds of times before, with the force of two g's pushing me down in the seat. The color of sky and ground interchanging, then returning to where they belonged.

Below, hundreds of acres and miles of cattle country in central Florida stretched out as far as the eye could see.

The edge of a puffy white cumulus cloud, looking like cotton, spread its thin vapor out touching the left wingtip of my new yellow and white Citabria. The thin mist curled around the wingtip looking like angel wings until they vanished like magic into the vast expanse of sky.

Memories of a C-46 cargo flight over the Andes Mountains in the pitch black of night with shafts of lightening flashing through the cockpit found me blinking my eyes as if a reflex to that brightness of long ago.

There would not be hundreds of spectators watching like the Homestead Airshow as I flew past them inverted at 800 feet with the engine shut down. This last landing at Placid

Lakes Airport, in Lake Placid, Florida, would be one of solitude.

A gentle wheel landing with the tires kissing the runway seemed to put an end to the flight as the small tail wheel slowly settled onto the runway.

Twenty-thousand hours of flight time had come to an end with that single landing. The slow cadence of the 115-horse power 0-235 played a familiar song as the plane turned off the paved runway and onto the grass leading to the hangar. As I opened the cockpit window, the aroma of fresh cut grass filled my senses. It was just like that first flight in the yellow J-3 Cub with Charlie Burr at Burr's Berry Farm many years ago.

In front of the hangar, the engine became quiet as I pulled the red knob of the mixture as I had done with my epileptic student to control altitude. The propeller turned one final blade as the last click from the impulse magneto signaled the end.

Within a few weeks of advertising in Barnstormers, someone showed interest. A buyer from Georgia arranged for a purchase date. The buyer arrived, paperwork was completed, and the Citabria's white and yellow Star Burst paint design flashed in the sunlight as we pushed it out of the darkness of the hangar.

Standing by the side of the plane, I watched the new owner fasten the seatbelt and adjust the shoulder harness as I had done so many times before.

"Clear prop!" came his request as I gave him a thumbs-up that all was indeed clear. The engine came to life and the new owner waved as he began a slow taxi over the grass to the 5,000-foot paved runway.

I watched the plane turn into position for takeoff at the far end of the runway. Sunlight once more flashed off the wing and fuselage. Within what seemed like seconds the Citabria raced by, lifted into the air, and climbed into the beautiful, blue Florida sky.

Standing there on the side of the runway, I watched as the yellow and white Citabria faded into gray, and then black, as the silhouette became smaller. Its engine faded into silence as the plane disappeared.

Walking back into the empty hangar, I picked up a broom and began sweeping the hangar floor for the new owner. The photos of aerobatic students, contests, and airshows were taken down from the walls and placed in a cardboard box along with the book that I had written, *The Art of Broomstick Flying*. The box was sealed and carried outside where I placed it on the passenger side of my Ford Ranger. Walking back to the empty hangar, I slid the hangar door closed. I walked back to the truck. The stickers on the truck's back window held their own history.

In large white letters were "www.betterpilot.com." Surrounding those large white letters were decals from the Experimental Aircraft Association, Aircraft Owners and Pilots Association, National Association of Flight Instructors, and the Seaplane Pilots Association. Those stickers, like myself, now seemed to have little value.

There had been no greater endeavor than teaching and sharing what I loved with others. That endeavor in the world that I loved so much had come to an end, with only three little words that were to control my future: I have cancer. In 2013, I was found to have prostate cancer.

Chapter Sixteen

I learned strange names like Cyberknife, Proton Radiation Therapy, Chemotherapy, Brachytherapy, Cryosurgery, prostatectomy, all words that I did not understand. Those terms that left doubt and confusion about the best path to take to survive cancer. Among those possibilities and strange words, I saw "Watchful Waiting." With this process, you simply wait and see if your cancer has progressed while continuing to receive biopsies and MRI treatments.

How does cancer grow and survive? Through some research, I discovered that cancer cannot live in an alkaline environment surrounded with oxygen. Doing further research, I found an alternative cure from the leaf and bark of the soursop tree a combination called Graviola. Early research showed that many years ago a leading university found that Graviola is 2,000 times more powerful than chemotherapy. Another amazing finding is that, unlike chemotherapy, it only targets the cancer cells. Since Graviola is a natural substance, it cannot hold a patent by pharmaceutical companies.

My oncologist was with a large university cancer center. He suggested that I begin with the university's Cancer Research Program. The advantage was that they would administer free MRI and biopsy tests. The Graviola was something that I had started taking so the test offered would see if it was doing any good.

While filling out a multitude of forms for their research, I asked, "Have you heard of Graviola or Soursop used in the treatment of cancer?"

My oncologist, in his white coat, turned away from me. He reached into the white cabinet in his examination room. Turning back, he held out his fist and then opened it. In his opened hand was a common rubber band.

"You might be able to prevent pregnancy if you use this," came his reply.

More research found that another oncologist claimed to have cured his own cancer using alternative medicine. He then prescribed it for his patients. He was arrested for malpractice, served five years in prison, fined, and lost his license to practice medicine.

Over the next six months, my experiment had begun. I started with thirty drops of Graviola in a cup of water taken twice a day and seven drops of Oxylift in a cup of water taken three times a day.

The day of the MRI and biopsy had arrived. The early morning sunlight flooded through the bedroom window announcing the new day, but for me it was a day filled with anxiety.

A strange thing was happening, although my mother had passed away years before, her voice was clear and strong. The melody of my mother's song seemed locked in my head. That song that she had sung to me in my baby highchair just after telling me to "open the hangar door."

"Praise God from whom all blessing flow

Praise Him all creatures here below
Praise Him above the heavenly host
Praise Father, Son, and Holy Ghost!"

Even after arriving at the University of Miami's Sylvester Comprehensive Cancer Center, mother's song, the Doxology, would not stop playing over and over in my mind. I completed the patient sign-in. Sitting down in a chair, I felt I was about to be reprimanded by my high school principal.

My legs were shaking and the room temperature felt like it was thirty degrees below zero. Mother's song started playing in my mind again. This time it was interrupted by a voice that called out when the Examination Room door opened, "Mixon."

Sitting down in the room waiting for the doctor, my apprehension and uneasiness took on a foreboding feeling of finality. Within minutes, I would be told how much the cancer had spread!

The oncologist walked into the room wearing his customary white coat. He sat down at his desk in front of me. The deathly still and silence of the room was finally broken with his words as he looked at the illuminated screen in front of him. "Let's see what we have here."

He concentrated on the bright screen while looking for the telltale signs of my cancer. He turned the illuminated screen toward me so that I could view the damage and better understand his evaluation. My foot was jittery against the floor as I waited for the news. Leaning toward him and the bright screen, the thought of what I was about to hear was overwhelming. My mind was racing with all the alternatives that I had researched in hopes of getting rid of cancer: Cyberknife, chemotherapy, cryosurgery, and all their side effects.

The oncologist began, "Here is the area." He pointed to the bright screen with his finger. "This is where it was. It is completely gone. No Cancer."

"What? Are you sure?"

"This is where it was," he said, pointing to the screen. "Now there is not even a trace of cancer."

It took me several hours to realize that what he had said was true. A former flight student of mine heard of my cancer and how it disappeared. Without my saying a word to him, he called and said, "Graviola." I asked how he knew. He said that three of his family members had used it. One with prostate cancer, one with lung cancer, and another with bone cancer. The prostate and lung cancers were cured completely. The bone cancer was cured by fifty percent.

It was time to find a flight school. It was time to fly and teach again.

While I was searching for employment at a flight school, another man was also searching. He was driving a rented Mitsubishi Galant from Alamo Rent-a-car and putting 3,836 miles on the car before returning it. His charisma, machismo, and utter confidence showed in his demeanor and the way he dressed. He was way above the ordinary car rental customer.

He wore chocolate-colored alligator skin-leather boots handmade by a bootmaker. The boots supposedly cost an unbelievable price tag of $12,995. To complement his boots, he wore a pair of Stefani Ricci cotton-blend dark blue jeans valued at $1,096 and a blue cashmere knit polo shirt that he purchased for only $898. On his right hand, he wore a large 3-carat men's diamond solitaire pinky ring for which he claimed to have paid $29,900.

He was born on September 1, 1968 and educated at Cairo University and Hamburg Technical University. His studies were in engineering and he graduated with a degree in architecture at the top of his class. His father did not allow him to socialize with other children when he was young, but kept him focused on his studies. His father was a lawyer and his mother, also well educated, was married at age 14 in an arranged marriage. His father was strict and private, and the whole family was considered reclusive. He was the only son, but he had two sisters in professional fields, one a medical doctor and the other a professor.

On March 22, 2000 while still in Germany, he sent this email to the academy of Lakeland, Florida inquiring about flight training:

Dear Sir,

We are a small group of young men from different Arab countries. Now we are living in Germany for a while to study. We would like to start training for the career of professional airline pilots. In this field, we haven't yet any knowledge but we are ready to undergo an intensive training program (up to ATP and eventually higher).

Fifty to sixty similar emails were sent to flight training schools in the United States. Johnelle Bryant, former loan officer at the U.S. Department of Agriculture in South Florida, stated that, just before his entry into the United States, he wanted to finance the purchase of a crop duster aircraft.

He and his friends entered the Accelerated Pilot Program at Huffman Aviation in Venice, Florida on Florida's west coast. They stayed with Hoffman's bookkeeper and his wife in the spare room of their house. After a week, they were asked to leave because they were rude.

Over the next several months, they had achieved both Commercial Pilot and Instrument Pilot ratings. From Huffman Aviation, they went to Eagle International for McDonnell Douglas DC-9 and Boeing 737-300 jet airline training at Opa-locka Airport in Miami, Florida where they practiced on a Boeing 727 simulator. They then attained 767 simulator training from Pan Am International. They purchased flight deck videos for the Boeing 747-200, Boeing 757-200, Airbus A320 and Boeing 767-300 ER models via mail order from Sporty's Pilot Shop in Batavia, Ohio.

So, there he was driving a rented plain white Mitsubishi Galant from Alamo Rental along State Road 80 leading into the small agriculture town of Belle Glade on the southern tip of Lake Okeechobee, Florida. In the distance, a massive column of gray smoke rose into the sky. The smoke came from a huge sugar corporation that had started their seasonal burn to prepare the 70,000 acres of sugar cane for harvest.

Passing a small group of framed houses in need of paint, he noticed the name of the development, "mud city," named after the rich, black soil that surrounded Belle Glade. He noticed many of the poorly maintained homes had laundry drying the old-fashioned way hung on clotheslines in the backyards. The sign on State Road 80 as he entered Belle Glade read: "Our wealth is in our soil," recalling the opposite expression "dirt poor."

The car pulled up to the intersection of State Road 80 and Gator Road. The name Gator was appropriate because within the 70,000 acres of sugar cane drainage canals were alligators. On the right side of the intersection down Gator Road was an airport. It had an east-west runway with five crop duster airplanes tied down next to the airstrip. Driving up to one of the planes, he got out of the car to talk to one of the mechanics working on a plane.

"We don't give flying lessons here," the mechanic said quickly while noticing the overdressed driver.

"Oh, I already know how to fly. I'm just interested in looking over these crop dusters."

"Well, you are welcome to look, but don't touch!" came another quick reply.

"What kinds of materials can you spray with them?"

"Anything you can fill in their spray tanks."

"Do you mind if I watch a few takeoffs and landings?"

"If you want to," the mechanic said impatiently.

"Do all crop dusters have tailwheels?"

"Yes, and you would need tailwheel instructions, but we don't give those here."

"Where might I get tailwheel instructions?"

"Various organizations have a list of flight instructors who offer instruction. You might even check with the Federal Aviation Administration."

The man in the expensive clothes stood next to the runway watching a few planes come in to land. They loaded up their spray tanks and took off again. He got back into his rented car and drove back through the massive sugar cane fields toward Miami.

Not too long after their meeting, I received a telephone call.

"Is this Rob Mixon?"

"Yes, it is."

"I would like to sign up to be checked out in a tailwheel airplane."

"I'm sorry, but I just sold my plane. In fact, I'm looking for a flight school so I can continue giving flight instructions," I explained.

"As soon as you start doing tailwheel instructions again, will you let me know?"

"Of course, what did you say your name was?"

"Mohamed Atta."

Approximately one month later on September 11th 2001, Atta along with his conspirators, Hani Hanjour and Abdulaziz al-Omarai, traveled to Boston where they boarded American Airlines Flight 11. Fifteen minutes into the flight, the team of hijackers attacked and Atta took over the controls. At 8:46 a.m., Atta managed to crash the Boeing 767 into the North Tower of the World Trade Center, killing all aboard as well as 1,600 civilians and first responders.

After 9/11, any airport receiving federal funding was required to have a fence and a security code on the gate to allow entrance. Without a tailwheel airplane, I never got to teach Atta about the crop dusters. I can see now that he might have tried using a crop duster to spray innocent people somewhere in the United States with chemical weapons like lethal nerve gas agents.

Chapter Seventeen

The August Florida heat baked the asphalt. My search for a flight school to teach students stick and rudder skills had begun.

Moving back to the east coast of Florida to be involved in the cancer research program at Sylvester Comprehensive Cancer Center was a frightening situation. Even with the cancer cured, there is always the fear that it may return.

There was no longer a reason not to begin flight instructing. It seemed as if my life was given a second chance to do what I loved—to once again become a certified flight instructor.

With my cancer cured, I began the search for a flight school where I could teach stick and rudder skills. I discovered South Wind Aviation. South Wind was a small flight school with a couple of older Cessna 152s and an even older Citabria to be used to teach aerobatics. The Citabria's red and white faded paint didn't come close to the colors on the one that I had sold.

Without my own airplane, I knew that, if I found a flight school, I would have to be checked out by their school's check pilot. In my case, the check pilot would be the flight school's owner.

The owner of the flight school had arranged to check my abilities to be a flight instructor, by disguising a dangerous situation in flight to see how I would react to it.

We arrived at the plane and he did the preflight checklist as I observed. Coming to the horizontal stabilizer, he raised the elevator by lifting the trim tab bringing it out of the neutral position for takeoff. This would make the airplane pitch up out of control.

"Rob, do you want to fly from the front seat or back?"

"Either is fine. Since I'll be instructing from the back, I'll fly from the backseat."

We climbed into the tandem seat configuration of the Citabria. The owner taxied to the runway. He completed the checklist for takeoff, but did not move the trim control back to neutral. The trim setting he had selected would pitch the nose up during our climb, possibly causing the plane to stall so that he would have to grab the controls to save us from crashing. Taxiing onto the active runway, he called out during the last second before flight, "your plane."

Not being able to reach the trim control with my hand since it was located next to his seat in front of me, I pushed the control forward into the neutral position with my left foot.

We raced down the runway with full power, engine thundering and the tail lifting for takeoff.

"Rob, do you need any help with that trim?"

"No, the trim is properly set for takeoff."

"How did you do that?"

"Left foot" came my reply.

The owner believed that the trim control, next to him in the front seat, was out of my reach.

At 4,000 feet, the checkout maneuvers began. The nose of the plane climbed into a power-on-stall, rapidly falling off into a three-turn spin. The vertical down line of the spin increased airspeed to 140 miles an hour and into a loop.

"Rob, I am afraid my flight instructor and his instruction was not as good as yours."

Three perfect landings and we were taxiing back toward South Wind Aviation and the hangar. The school's owner was eager to share his new toy with me.

"Rob, have you ever flown a Stearman?"

"I have a few hours in one."

"Have you flown one with 450 horsepower?"

"That would be the one."

We walked over in the dim hangar light toward a beautiful 450-horsepower Stearman biplane. The plane looked as if it had just returned from the factory and appeared in new condition.

"Rob, the Stearman just had a complete recover and engine overhaul. I want to put at least ten hours on her with someone before flying her solo. Would you mind flying with me?"

"Sure, not a problem."

"Do you have time today?"

"I'll make time."

Reaching into the cockpit, I found a pair of goggles and a cloth khaki-colored flying cap, along with a checkered, creased, and worn leather flight jacket. The flying cap was sitting on top of the control stick. We pushed the plane out of the dim hangar into the bright Florida sun.

Sitting in the open cockpit, I felt an adrenaline rush when the deep-throated sound of the 450-horsepower radial engine belched a puff of white smoke as it roared to life.

Lined up for takeoff, we added full power. The Stearman raced down the runway, tail up with the sound of the 450-horsepower engine thundering across the airport's open field echoing against the side of the metal hangars. The wind filled the cockpit. Reaching up, I adjusted the cloth cap and flight goggles. We headed east toward the coast.

In the distance, the deep blue water of the Gulf Stream looked like hundreds of seagulls as the white-capped waves merged into the dark blue ocean.

Looking south, I saw the white building on the shoreline that was once the terminal for Pan American World Airways and their seaplanes. That terminal where people like Winston Churchill and famous movie stars had flown on Pan Am's "Clipper ships" to exotic places. That place where my mother and I watched my father arrive in those S-42 seaplanes, with mother holding me up over the observation deck's retaining wall.

"There he is! There he is!" she would shout as my father walked up to the terminal from the seaplanes.

Farther south were the steppingstone islands of the Florida Keys. The bright aqua and deep blue waters of the Keys were still a monument to Charles Henry and a time when people were more independent and self-sufficient.

Hundreds of miles farther south near the equator were the Andes Mountains. Those mountains with their tall peaks, dark turbulent nights, sending blinding shafts of lightening into the cockpit as if guarding the entrance to Lima, Peru and a small airport on the other side of the equator called Talara.

Looking over the left side of the open cockpit, I could see the Crandon Park Bridge. The white caps were not unlike the day when a young fourteen-year-old boy went sailing to explore his skill and expertise during small craft warnings.

Pushing the Stearman's left rudder and stick, I flew right near the bridge which was now directly in front of the plane. The plane descended to 500 feet, with reduced power.

Once more adjusting my flying cap and goggles, I looked over the right side of the open cockpit. The yellow biplane had US NAVY in black letters under the bottom of the lower wings. Round military stars were on both sides of the fuselage and out by each wing tip. Red stripes were on top of the wings just inboard of the wing stars. The Stearman had a blue painted rudder matching the blue surrounding the military stars with their red centers. All of this brought back another time when as a young boy I first saw a similar Stearman in this very spot and realized that I had to be a pilot.

The huge propeller sliced through the air. The deep-throated sound of the radial engine echoed off the bridge below. Raising my right arm with the checkered, creased, and worn leather flight jacket, I placed my fingers together into a salute. It was a salute to the open, sandy, space below where once I had stood as a boy looking up.

The rhythmic beat of the 450-horsepower engine and rush of outside air into the open cockpit, reminded me once again of my mother singing her song,

"Praise God, from whom all blessing flow."

Epilogue

The green and white rotating beacon at New Tamiami Airport, now called Miami-Executive Airport, flashed its laser colors into the night.

Clean, white, business jets spooled up their engines for taxi, following the blue taxiway lights to runway Nine Right as they prepared for takeoff.

The red glow of cockpit lights slowly merged with the orange glow and pink clouds of sunrise. Pilots followed directions from the control tower, acknowledging their instructions, as earth once again saw the dawn of early morning light.

"24 Charlie, cleared for takeoff."

"Roger, 24 Charlie, cleared for takeoff. Request a straight-out departure."

"24 Charlie, straight-out approved. Good day."

A student stood with his flight instructor, on the ramp near a flight school next to a red and white Cessna.

With the preflight inspection completed, they stood next to the Cessna's open door. The student reached down to the white paper attached to a clipboard that was strapped to his left leg.

With the first question of the day, the student asked, "What is the stall speed of this airplane?"

His flight instructor with a slight grin on her face replied, "Don't know; never looked."

Forty years later while on a charter flight to San Juan, Puerto Rico:

The overnight hotel room was in the Condado Plaza Hilton in Old San Juan. The old Spanish architecture of the surrounding buildings and the narrow brick-paved streets were only out done by the view of the Atlantic Ocean from the hotel window.

From the hotel room on the narrow streets below along Condado Boulevard, ladies of the evening could be seen walking around as soon as the sun went down. The flight crews referred to them as "Condado Commandos." Six months ago, there had been an incident when a co-pilot from a major airline was lured into the barrios, only to be beaten and robbed.

The following morning at Luis Munoz Maren International Airport the preflight inspection had been completed after the plane had been refueled. Bright pink clouds were blowing in from the ocean in the sunrise at 7:34.

Ground Control was tuned in at 121.9 and taxi instructions received to proceed to runway 26. Arriving at the active runway, the frequency was changed to the tower frequency of 132.05.

"November 248 Zulu cleared for takeoff."

"Tower 48 Zulu cleared for takeoff, requesting a left turn out northwest bound.

"48 Zulu, left turn approved. Contact Departure Control at 119.4."

"119.4," came the reply to the tower, acknowledging the instructions.

"48 Zulu, have a good flight."

The water below sparkled in the sunlight as November 48 Zulu climbed and then leveled off at 10,000 feet. The blue sea and sky seemed to have no horizon. White puffy cumulous clouds floated over the sea below.

In the peaceful space at 10,000 feet, I thought about what things had become and what things could have been. The lyrics and tune from the hymn *It Is Well* flowed through my mind.

"When peace like a riv-er, at-tend-eth my way,
When sor-rows like sea bil-lows roll; what-ev-er
My lot, thou has taught me to say, it is well,
It is well with my soul."

In the relative quiet of the jet's cockpit, compared to the old C-46 piston engine cargo flights, I looked over at the young co-pilot who looked like a high school teenager. My thoughts moved from the lyrics of the hymn to a feeling that I once had for Savannah Ann Cooper. Watching her go through her struggle to survive, I remembered her as a skinny kid in elementary school. She had once given me a game of Jax (six jacks and a small ball) as a classroom Christmas present. My thoughts turned to how she came in Third Place. She felt she had won a major victory in an aerobatic contest. She stood taller and felt at ease with her accomplishment.

Remembering her quote from Tigger, I laughed and blurted out, "Once in a while someone amazing comes along, and here I am."

With a puzzled look, my copilot asked, "What?"

"Never mind. It is well with my soul," I replied.

That once little gangly kid in elementary school who bloomed into a supermodel and who brightened up the room with her personality and smile, that kid who had soloed an airplane and had done precision spins for a flight instructor on only a student pilot's license, Savannah Ann Cooper, the love of my life, would be waiting for me at home.

The Transition

She's just a young girl short on pride
Her parents tell her to abide…
"You'll fail that test; don't even try."
She feels her stomach knot inside

Then one day she takes a ride
With flight instructor by her side,
they soar the clouds, look down on earth
and deep inside, she feels the birth…
of confidence and sense of worth

Now with controls in her command,
She flies a plane high over land…
That land that told her she could not
Those words below that she forgot

For now, she flies at one with earth,
and with new spirit given birth
With flight instructor by her side
She finds within her lasting pride

She took control and ruled the skies
No longer a young girl short on pride
And when they landed on that day
A new young captain walked away!

Rob Mixon

APPENDIX A

Flight Instructor Award

Flight Instructor of the Year awarded by Flight Standards District office, Miami, Florida after publishing my book entitled *The Art of Broomstick Flying: Techniques of Pre-Solo Flight*.

Department of Transportation
Federal Aviation Administration
Flight Instructor of the Year

Robert G. Mixon

1994 District Winner

THIS AWARD IS ISSUED AS RECOGNITION OF YOUR SUSTAINED SUPERIOR PERFORMANCE AS A LEADER IN THE FIELD OF AVIATION SAFETY THROUGH YOUR CONTINUED PILOT TRAINING AS A CERTIFIED FLIGHT INSTRUCTOR AND AS AN ADJ PROFESSOR IN THE AVIATION DEPARTMENT OF THE MIAMI DADE COMMUNITY COLLEGE.

September 8, 1994

DATE

MIAMI FSDO 19
OFFICE MANAGER

APPENDIX B

The Wright Brothers "Master Pilot" Award
Awarded for 20,000 hours of flight time and professionalism in promoting aviation safety.

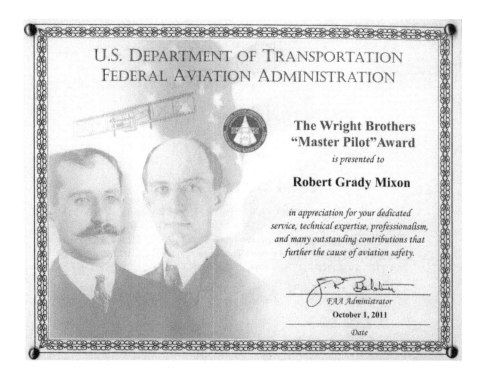

Author Rob Mixon in a Pitts Special before painting the traditional red and white Pitts paint scheme.

GLOSSARY

Aileron
a hinged control surface on the wing to aid in producing a bank or rolling about the longitudinal axis.

Airfoil
any member or surface on an airplane whose major function is to deflect the airflow.

Airplane
a mechanically driven flying machine which derives its lift from the reaction of the mass of air which is deflected downward by fixed wings.

Airport
a tract of land or water which has been established as a landing area for the regular use of aircraft.

Airspeed
the speed of an airplane in relation to the air through which it is passing.

Airworthy

the status of being in condition suitable for safe flight.

Altimeter

an instrument for indicating the relative altitude of an airplane by measuring atmospheric pressure.

Altitude

the elevation of an airplane. The altitude may be specified as above sea level or above the ground which it flies over.

Attitude

the position of an airplane considering the inclination of its axis in relation to the horizon.

Angle of attack

the wind coming toward the front of the wing is called Relative Wind. When the wing is moved up in relation to the relative wind, the distance between the wing and the wind is called the Angle of Attack. If this distance gets too great, it is said to be an "excessive angle of attack" and a stall will result until the angle of attack is lessened by releasing the control stick or control yoke so that the nose of the airplane is lowered into the relative wind. Although the airspeed will drop lower, it is this excessive angle of attack that will cause the airplane to stall at any speed no matter how fast the airplane is flying. A misconception is that an airplane will stall because it runs out of airspeed when the excessive angle of attack is causing the plane to run out of airspeed and stall, not the airspeed indicator.

NOTE: although the airspeed may drop during an excessive angle of attack, it is the excessive angle of attack that causes the aerodynamic stall. An airplane may be stalled at any airspeed.

Axis
the theoretical line extending through the center of gravity of an airplane in each major plane: fore and aft, crosswise, and up and down. These are the longitudinal, lateral, and vertical axes.

Bank
to tip or roll about the longitudinal axis of the airplane. Banks are incumbent to all properly executed turns.

Biplane
an airplane having two main supporting surfaces with one above the other.

Canopy
the main supporting surface of the parachute.

Ceiling
(meteorology) the height of the base of the clouds above the ground.

Ceiling
(aircraft) the maximum altitude the airplane can obtain under standard conditions.

Center of gravity

the point within an airplane through which, for balance purposes, the total force of gravity is considered to act.

Checklist

a list, usually carried in the pilot's compartment, of items requiring the airman's attention for various flight operations.

Checkpoint

In air navigation, a prominent landmark on the ground, either visible, radio, or GPS, which is used to establish the position of an airplane in flight.

Cockpit

an open space in the fuselage with seats for the pilot and passengers; used also to denote the pilot's compartment in a large airplane.

Compass (magnetic)

a device for determining the direction of the earth's magnetic field. It is subject to local disturbances, but the compass will indicate the direction to the north magnetic pole.

Control surfaces

hinged airfoils exposed to the airflow which control the attitude of the airplane and which are activated by using the controls in the airplane.

Control stick

is used in combination with the rudder pedals to make a coordinated turn.

Control yoke
is used for the same purpose as the control stick, but looks like an automobile steering wheel.

Controls
the devices used by a pilot in operating an airplane.

Coordination
the movement or use of two or more controls in their proper relationship to obtain the results desired.

Cushioning (ground effect)
the temporary gain in lift during a landing due to the compression of the air between the wings of an airplane and the ground.

Drag
force opposing the motion of the airplane through the air.

Elevator
a hinged, horizontal control surface used to raise or lower the tail in flight.

Empennage
term used to designate the entire tail group of an airplane, including the fixed and movable tail surfaces.

Fin
a fixed airfoil to increase the stability of an airplane, usually applied to the vertical surface to which the rudder is hinged (vertical stabilizer).

Final approach
the last segment of the flight just before landing.

Flap
an appendage to an airfoil, usually the wing, for changing its lift characteristics to permit slower landings.

Flare out (landing flare)
to round out a landing by decreasing the rate of descent and airspeed by slowly raising the nose.

Flight plan
a detailed outline of a proposed flight usually filed with an airways communications station before cross country flight.

Front
the line of demarcation between two different types of air mass.

Fuselage
the body to which the wings, landing gear, and tail are attached.

Glide
sustained forward flight in which speed is maintained only by the loss of altitude.

Ground loop
an uncontrollable violent turn on the ground.

Horsepower

a unit of measurement of power output of an engine. It is the power required to raise 550 pounds one foot in one second.

Inverted

flying upside down.

Landing

the act of terminating flight and bringing the airplane to rest, used both for land and seaplanes.

Landing area

any area suitable for the landing of an airplane.

Leading edge

the forward edge of an airfoil.

Landing gear

the under structure which supports the weight of the airplane while at rest.

Lift

the supporting force induced by the dynamic reaction of air against the wing.

Light gun

an intense, narrowly-focused spotlight with which a green, red, or white signal may be directed at any selected airplane in the traffic on or about an airport.

Log
to make a flight-by-flight record of all operations of an airplane, engine, or pilot, listing flight time, are of operation, and other pertinent information.

Loop
flying vertically up, then upside-down, diving back toward the earth, ending up in right-side-up level flight, and terminating in right-side-up level flight.

Maneuver
any planned motion of an airplane in the air or on the ground.

Overshoot
to fly beyond the designated area or mark.

Pilot
one who operates the controls of the airplane in flight.

Pitot tube
a tube exposed to the airstream for maneuvering impact pressure or for measuring outside undisturbed static pressure. It measures that pressure on the airspeed indicator.

Pitch (airplane)
angular displacement about any line.

Rig
adjustment of the airfoils of an airplane to produce desired flight characteristics.

Roll

displacement around the longitudinal axis of an airplane.

Rudder

has foot pedals that keep the airplane going straight on the ground and keeps the plane in a coordinated turn in the air when used in conjunction with the control stick or control yoke.

Rudder pedals

controls within the airplane by means of which the rudder is activated; two foot pedals for each foot to steer the plane on the ground and matched with the control stick or yoke in flight to make a coordinated turn.

Runway

a strip, either paved or improved, on which takeoffs and landings are effected.

Skid

Sideward motion of an airplane in flight and produced by centrifugal force.

Slip (or sideslip)

the controlled flight of an airplane in a direction not in line with its longitudinal axis.

Stick

the term used for the control stick in an aircraft that does not have a control yoke.

Snap roll

an aerial maneuver in which an aircraft rapidly turns upside down and then rapidly returns to right side up around its longitudinal axis.

Solo

a flight during which a pilot is the only occupant of the airplane.

Spin

is a stall with the control stick held back, keeping the airplane in a stall and adding full rudder in the direction you want the airplane to rotate. Recovery is power off, opposite rudder to stop the rotation, and relax or push forward on the control stick to break the stall.

Spiral

a prolonged gliding turn which at least 360 degrees change of direction is affected.

Stability

the tendency of an airplane in flight to remain in straight, level upright flight or to return to this attitude of displaced without attention of the pilot.

Stabilizer

the fixed airfoil of an airplane used to increase stability; usually the aft fixed horizontal surface to which the elevators are hinged.

Stall

When the wing is pulled into too steep of an upward angle, the lift moves too far back to hold the plane in the air and a stall occurs.

Tail slide

rearward motion of an airplane in the air commonly occurring only in a whip stall.

Tail wheel

a smaller wheel situated under the airplane used for directional control on the ground.

Tandem seating

is seating configuration for a two-place (pilot and passenger) airplane with one person in front of the other.

Taxi

to operate an airplane under its own power on the ground, (except when that movement is used for takeoff and landing).

Thermal

air rising from the ground due to being heated by the sun.

Thrust

the forward force of an airplane in the air provided by the engine acting through a propeller or jet engine.

Visibility

the greatest horizontal distance where prominent objects on the ground can be seen (used to denote weather conditions).

Wind shift

an abrupt change in the direction or velocity, or both, of the wind.

Windsock

a tapered cloth open at both ends and mounted aloft at an airport used to detect wind direction and general intensity (velocity).

Wing

an airfoil whose major function is to provide lift by the dynamic reaction of the mass of air swept downward causing a low-pressure area on top of the wing.

Wing tip

the end of the wing furthest from the fuselage or cabin.

Yaw

to turn about the vertical axis. (An airplane is said to yaw as the nose turns without the accompanying appropriate bank.)

Yoke

the term used for the steering wheel that initiates the bank or turn to be coordinated with the rudder control for a coordinated turn.

ENGINE OPERATION

Aircraft throttle

controls and regulates fuel flow. Regulates power or speed of the airplane; sometimes called a thrust lever in a jet engine aircraft.

Carburetor heat (carb heat)

a system used to prevent or clear carburetor icing. It consists of a moveable flap which draws hot air into the engine intake from the exhaust manifold.

Magneto

an electrical generator that keeps the ignition independent of the rest of the electrical system ensuring that the engine continues running in the event of alternator or battery failure.

Mixture control

is the red-colored knob that cuts fuel off from the engine to stop the engine from running by starving it of fuel.

.

ABOUT THE AUTHOR

Rob Mixon is an award-winning poet and writer. His work has been published in *Sport Aviation*, *Aviation Historian*, *Sport Aerobatics*, *Mentor*, *Vintage Aircraft*, and other publications. He was awarded the Department of Transportation, Federal Aviation Administration "Flight Instructor of the Year" in 1994 after publishing his book entitled *The Art of Broomstick Flying: Techniques of Pre-Solo Flight*. Rob was also awarded "The Wright Brothers Master Pilot Award" by the FAA for his "dedication, technical expertise, professionalism, and contribution to aviation safety."

There were other awards: "Most Authentic Aircraft Restoration" by the Historical Association of Southern Florida in 1977 at The Harvest: A Country Fair." Rob won First Place in both Spot Landings and Short Field Landings in 1983 at Bob and Suzi Harpers' "Cane Raisin' Fly-in" at Clewiston, Florida.

Achieving his degrees in Aviation and Education from Miami Dade College, he eventually taught aviation there as an Adjunct Professor in the Aviation Department. He also obtained his Bachelor's degree in Education from Florida International University and his Master's degree in Counseling from Barry University. While working on completing his education, Rob was employed by Pan Am as an Interior Aircraft Cleaner on 727 and 707 aircraft.

Later, Rob got to fly the L1011 aircraft while working for Eastern Airlines as a Cockpit Procedures Trainer in both the 727 and L1011 aircraft.

His interest in flying began as a young boy watching with his mother in the Pan American World Airway base in Coconut Grove, Florida as his father returned from far away exotic places on the Pan American S-42 seaplanes that were state of the art flying machines in the 1940s.

Rob has flown in aerobatic competition and airshows, earning the following ratings: Certified Flight Instructor Airplane and Instruments, Single Engine Land, Multiengine Land, Multiengine Sea, Airline Transport Pilot, and Glider Ratings with a total flight time of 20,000 hours.

This is the Chanute hang glider from the 1909 design.

THE GLIDER EXPERIMENT

Three early gliding pioneers were killed in glider crashes: Otto Lillenthal, Percy Pilcher, and John Montgomery. The glider is inferior for training and doesn't compare to today's modern hang gliders. Durations of flight were usually only a few seconds and only just above the ground, unless someone made the fatal mistake of jumping off a cliff. The distance flown was usually only several hundred feet.

Obtaining Federal Aviation Administration certification to make it a real aircraft required being given the registration number "N2579."

Sitting at the FAA inspector's desk, we began to fill out the "Aircraft Project File." The inspector began to ask the necessary questions as he filled out the form.

"How do you intend to launch this glider?" the inspector asked.

There was silence. I thought about the glider launching instruction that I had read about in an old *Popular Mechanics* magazine published in 1909.

"Will you launch by an airplane tow?" he asked next.

"No, I'm afraid that would be disastrous."

"Okay," said the inspector. "What will be your method of launch?"

"Well, the only two methods of launch established for a hang glider back in 1909 were to "leap into the air" or "jump of a cliff," I said.

The inspector got up from his chair, walked out of the room, and I could hear the laughter next door before he returned once again, composed and looking very professional.

The glider had antique gold-colored registration numbers outlined in black, along with a red, white, and blue American flag painted on the empennage, the translucent Dacron covering the wings and tail sections, and all the bracing and flying wires, the glider certainly looked like aviation had stepped back into the year 1909.

I tried on the glider by climbing into the twelve-inch elongated opening in the center of the bottom wing while I was surrounded with a 20-foot wing span. It felt like I was wearing an authentic antique replica.

My good friends had invited the local television station and newspapers to document the attempt of my first homemade glider flight.

It took some time to find a thirty-foot "cliff" in the flat land of South Florida, but we selected a pile of coral rock at a construction site for the adventure. The first takeoff started "beautiful." Clearing the edge of the cliff and obtaining flight, I got ready to control and maneuver the glider by shifting my body weight just as they did in the "good ol' days."

I heard the CRACK sound as the tail hit the edge of the cliff, causing me and the glider to point toward the ground below.

Television cameras rolled catching the action and failure.

The second takeoff became a reality. Once again hanging in space with apparently good lift.

CRACK. The edge of the thirty-foot cliff got in the way again. There was a loss of lift. Suddenly, the jagged coral rocks and the rocky protrusions were in front of me.

The glider picked up enough speed before hitting the ground, putting the brunt force of the landing on my right ankle.

That night on the local television stations news I watched myself crawling out from the twelve-inch elongated opening in the bottom wing, covered with dirt and limping on my right ankle.

The *South Dade Leader* newspaper the next day had me pictured on the front page standing on the edge of the small cliff wearing the hang glider N2579.

The crutches and severe sprain taught me a realistic lesson about what aviation was like back in 1909.

PILOT'S SPIRIT

How could a pilot an atheist be...
Who travels the heavens, looks down on the sea...
Observes the creation of moisture-turned clouds.
Of lightning's fire and thunder clapped cloud.

To rise in a thermal, hang under a cloud,
Then land on a mountain field newly plowed...
To listen to sounds from a babbling brook
As it flows from the mountains where he lands to look.

Then with an urge to lose earthly bounds,
He climbs in his airplane and lifts from the ground...
Invisible lift that takes him on high,
He travels the heavens we mortals call sky.

Rob Mixon
The Art of Broomstick Flying

Made in United States
Orlando, FL
03 March 2023

30665748R00095